CONTEMPORARY

INTERMEDIATE 1

reading
basics

A REAL-WORLD APPROACH TO LITERACY

McGraw Hill Education

Bothell, WA • Chicago, IL • Columbus, OH • New York, NY

www.mheonline.com

 **Education**

Send all inquiries to:
Contemporary/McGraw-Hill
130 East Randolph Street, Suite 400
Chicago, IL 60601

ISBN: 978-0-07-658370-6
MHID: 0-07-658370-8

Printed in the United States of America.

5 6 7 8 9 QVS 17 16 15 14

Contents

UNIT 1

Lesson 1.1

Lesson 1.2

Lesson 1.3

Lesson 1.4

Lesson 1.5

Lesson 1.6

Lesson 1.7

UNIT 2

Lesson 2.1

Lesson 2.2

To the Student

Reading Basics will help you become a better reader. Research in evidence-based reading instruction (EBRI) has shown that reading has four important components, or parts: comprehension, alphabetics, vocabulary, and fluency. *Reading Basics* provides evidence-based reading instruction and practice in all four components. With your teacher's help, you can use the *Student Edition* and the articles in the *Intermediate 1 Reader* to gain important skills.

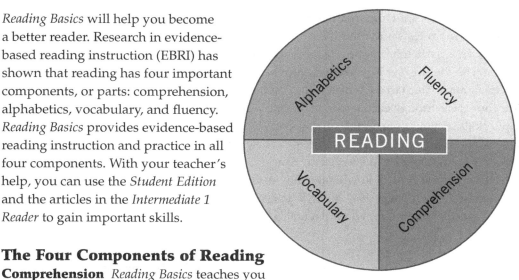

The Four Components of Reading

Comprehension *Reading Basics* teaches you many ways to improve your reading comprehension. Each lesson in the *Student Edition* introduces a different reading comprehension skill. You apply the skill to passages and to a workplace document. You also apply the skill to the articles in the *Reader*. Your teacher will help you use monitoring and fix-up reading strategies. You will learn ways to clarify your understanding of passages that are confusing to you. In addition, each article in the *Reader* begins with a before-reading strategy. At the end of the article, you will complete comprehension and critical thinking exercises.

Alphabetics In the *Student Edition* lessons, you will learn and practice alphabetics. Alphabetics includes phonics and word analysis skills, such as recognizing long and short vowels and syllable patterns, correctly spelling plurals and possessives, and studying word parts, such as prefixes, suffixes, and base words. You can use alphabetics skills to help you read and understand difficult words. For more practice, go to www.mhereadingbasics.com and use *PassKey*. This online program provides skills instruction and guided feedback.

Vocabulary Studying academic vocabulary will help you as a learner. Your teacher will present and explain five academic vocabulary words that you will need to understand as you read each *Student Edition* lesson. You will have a chance to practice these words along with other important vocabulary skills such as recognizing and using synonyms, antonyms, and context clues.

Your teacher will also present and explain vocabulary words important to your understanding of the articles in the *Reader*. As you read each article, notice that some words are defined in the margins. Use the definition and the context of each word to help you understand it.

Fluency Your teacher will present activities to help you with fluency—that is, reading smoothly, quickly, and accurately. You will practice fluency with the passages in the *Student Edition* and the articles in the *Reader*. You can also go to www.mhereadingbasics.com to download MP3 recordings of the articles. Listening to fluent reading will help you develop your own fluency skills.

How to Use This Book

The *Student Edition* consists of 19 lessons split among three units. These lessons help prepare you for questions on classroom tests and on important assessments. Each lesson is eight pages long and focuses on a particular reading comprehension skill.

Begin by taking the Pretest. Use the Answer Key to check your answers. Circle any wrong answers and use the Evaluation Chart to see which skills you need to practice.

Your teacher will guide your class through each lesson in the book. You will have chances to practice and apply skills on your own and in small groups. At the end of each unit, complete the Unit Review and Assessment. The Assessment will help you check your progress. Your teacher may want to discuss your answers with you.

After you complete the lessons in the book, you will take the Posttest on pages 189–198. The Evaluation Chart and Answer Key on pages 199–200 will help you see how well you have mastered the skills. To achieve mastery, you must answer 80 percent of the questions correctly.

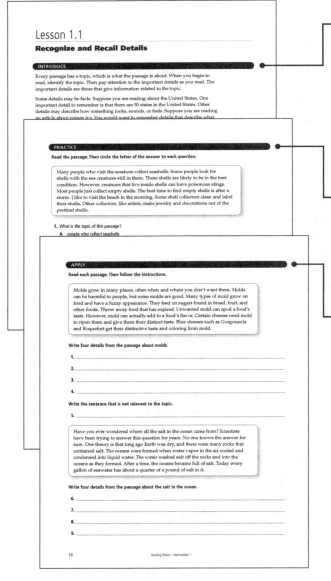

Working through Each Lesson

Introduce The first page of each lesson presents the reading skill. It also includes an example. Your teacher will use this example to explain and model the skill. Then your teacher will work with your class to do the guided practice at the bottom of the page. You will have a chance to practice this skill in the activities. Later in the lesson you will apply this skill to a document similar to one that you might use in the workplace.

Practice Next comes a page for practice. Usually, you will read a passage and answer questions about it that relate to the reading skill. You may be asked to fill out a graphic organizer to respond to a question. On some pages, there will be several passages followed by questions.

Apply The Apply page gives you a chance to apply the reading skill in a different way. In many lessons, you will read a passage and answer questions about it. You will see a variety of formats, including open-ended questions and graphic organizers.

Check Up The last page in the reading skills section of the lesson is the Check Up page. The questions on this page are always presented in a multiple-choice format. The Check Up page allows your teacher to monitor your progress as you learn the reading skill. Then your teacher can help you if you still have questions about the skill.

Workplace Skill The Workplace Skill page gives you another chance to practice the reading skill. Instead of using a reading passage, this page introduces the types of documents that you might find or need to use in the workplace. There could be a memo, a section of a handbook, or some kind of graph. You will read or study the document and answer questions about it.

The Workplace Skill documents relate to a wide variety of jobs. Some may be familiar to you, while others may be new.

Write for Work A Write for Work activity is at the top of the next page. You will do workplace-related writing such as drafting an e-mail or a memo. The writing relates to the document on the Workplace Skill page. This activity provides a chance for you to practice your writing skills and reading comprehension at the same time.

Reading Extension In most lessons, a Reading Extension comes next. Here you apply the reading skill to an article in the *Reader*. After reading the article, you will answer multiple-choice and open-ended questions.

Workplace Extension Some lessons have a Workplace Extension instead of a Reading Extension. The Workplace Extension addresses work-related issues. These might include dealing with the first day on a job or responding appropriately to a boss. You will read a scenario in which a person is faced with a work problem or issue. Then you will answer questions about how the person handled the situation or what he or she should do next.

For each unit, your teacher will hand out a Workplace Skill Activity sheet. You will work with a partner or in small groups to practice skills similar to those in the Workplace Extension. Many of these activities include role-playing so that you can practice realistic conversations about the workplace.

Workplace Skill:
Understand Author's Purpose in an Employee Memo

Employers use memos to give information about their company plans and policies. They also use memos to describe company procedures. Memos always have a specific purpose. A memo should have the name of the sender and the name of the recipient or recipients. It should also include the subject and the date.

Read the memo. Then circle the letter of the answer to each question below the box.

MEMO

To: Employees of Peyton Discount Stores
From: Samantha Peyton, Owner of Peyton Discount Stores
Date: January 30

Subject: Shoplifting Reminders

There was a shoplifting attempt in the hardware department of our Louisville store last month. This is a good opportunity to remind you about our company's procedures. We have established guidelines for handling a suspected shoplifter in our stores.

In a situation in which a suspected shoplifter is still present in the store, follow these guidelines: Make every effort to delay his or her departure from the store. This will allow time for the proper authorities to arrive at the scene. However, at no time should your safety be at risk. Do not confront, accuse, or physically prevent the suspect from leaving the scene.

If a shoplifter leaves the store, follow these guidelines: Remain inside the store. If you are able to see the suspect's vehicle, take note of its make, model, and license-plate number. Attempt to assess the physical appearance of the suspect. This includes, but is not limited to, height, weight, hair color, and any other distinguishing physical features. Also note details about the suspect's clothing. Report this information to your store manager.

Your cooperation with these procedures is greatly appreciated.

1. What is the main purpose of business memos?   2. The author's intention for writing this memo is to

---

Write for Work

Your manager has asked you to write a memo or an e-mail about an upcoming company picnic. The picnic will be held on the grounds of Playland State Park. Think about what details you need to include in the memo. What do your fellow employees need to know? Think about your purpose for writing and about what should be included in a well-written memo. Write the memo in a notebook.

Reading Extension

Turn to "Escape to Freedom" on page 73 of *Reading Basics Intermediate 1 Reader*. After you have read and/or listened to the article, answer the questions below.

Circle the letter of the answer to each question.

1. What do you think the author's intention was for writing this article?
   A to describe Douglass's achievements as a free man
   B to convince readers that slavery is wrong
   C to describe the rough conditions of slavery
   D to tell how Douglass became free

2. What is the effect of the language in paragraph 14?
   F a feeling of anger
   G a feeling of suspense
   H a feeling of sadness
   J a feeling of happiness

3. What is the purpose of paragraphs 5 and 6?
   A to entertain readers with details of Douglass's trip
   B to persuade readers that "free papers" are important
   C to explain how Douglass planned to get papers and escape
   D to describe what it was like to be an American sailor

Write the answer to each question.

Write for Work

Your company is giving a presentation to employees on past trends in the California milk industry. To prepare for this, they have asked you to present information on milk sales. Use the graph on page 122 to analyze what was happening in milk sales in California. Write this information in a notebook.

Workplace Extension

The Presentation

Shelia O'Connell works for a local food and agricultural agency. She was asked to give a presentation on trends in the California milk industry. She was nervous. She had never presented information to a large group before. She did not have a great deal of time to prepare and practice. The conference was just a week away. She decided to make a plan. First she would take time to analyze the current trends in the industry. Then she would organize her information in a slideshow presentation. Finally, she would do a practice presentation for a friend and ask for critical feedback on her performance.

Circle the letter of the answer to each question.

1. How would you consider Shelia's overall preparation for the presentation?
   A Her plan was poorly organized and thoughtless.
   B Her plan was well organized and planned.
   C Her plan did not take time to analyze the trends.
   D She did not organize her information in a productive way.

2. Was it important for Shelia to practice her presentation before a friend?
   F Yes; she and her friend could have a lot of fun and laughs that way.
   G No; it would not help her to make a better presentation.
   H No; she felt comfortable speaking to large groups.
   J Yes; she could get critical feedback on her performance.

Write the answer to the question.

3. What might happen if Shelia does not practice her slideshow presentation?

_____

_____

_____

Lesson 26   123

Explore Words You will practice two important reading skills in the Explore Words section of the lesson—alphabetics and vocabulary.

Each Explore Words section includes four or five activities. Each activity begins with brief instruction followed by practice. You may be asked to complete matching exercises, circle word parts, fill in missing words, or divide words into syllables.

Here are some of the alphabetics skills that you will practice:
- *r*-controlled vowels, vowel combinations
- consonant blends, hard and soft *c* and *g*
- possessives and contractions
- plurals and other word endings
- prefixes, suffixes, and base words
- syllable patterns

You will also practice vocabulary skills, such as these:
- context clues
- multiple-meaning words
- antonyms
- synonyms

In every lesson you will also work with the five academic vocabulary words your teacher will present before you begin reading the lesson. These words appear in context in the lesson. The Academic Vocabulary activity presents definitions of the words. You will use the words to complete sentences.

As you progress through the *Student Edition* lessons, you will notice improvements in your reading comprehension, alphabetics, vocabulary, and fluency skills. You will be a stronger and more confident reader.

Pretest

Read each passage. Then circle the letter of the answer to each question.

> Sometimes gardening and self-defense go hand in hand. That is true in the case of the spider crab. The spider crab is a saltwater species that lives on the sea bottom. This little crab makes a disguise with a "garden" of seaweed on its own shell. First it snips some small pieces of seaweed. Then it arranges the pieces carefully on its shell. Soon the seaweed covers the whole crab. From then on, the spider crab can hide from its enemies under its own "garden."

1. Which of the following concepts was stated in the passage?

   A   The spider crab is a clever creature.

   B   The spider crab can live on land.

   C   Spider crabs help gardens grow.

   D   The spider crab lives on the sea bottom.

2. As used in this passage, *disguise* means

   F   "a way to cover itself."

   G   "a place to grow food."

   H   "a pattern."

   J   "a gathering place."

3. From this passage, you can conclude that

   A   the spider crab's enemies are fooled by the "garden."

   B   the spider crab spins a web in the water.

   C   spider crabs can be found in forests.

   D   the spider crab's enemies are afraid of plants.

> White dwarfs are a type of small star. At one time, these stars were huge and red. They were known as red giants. Red giants eventually collapse in on themselves. What remains is a much smaller star with much of the mass of the larger one. In fact, some white dwarfs are about one million times as dense as water. That means that if it were on Earth, a one-inch cube of the white dwarf would weigh about 18 tons.

4. What is the main idea of this passage?

   F   White dwarfs were once huge, red stars.

   G   Some stars are smaller than other stars.

   H   White dwarfs are small but incredibly dense stars.

   J   Stars are denser than water.

5. The author's purpose for writing this passage is to

   A   persuade the reader to learn more about stars.

   B   inform readers about the best time to view stars.

   C   entertain readers with a story about space.

   D   describe white dwarfs.

Where did the sandwich get its name? The sandwich was named for John Montagu, the fourth Earl of Sandwich in England. Montagu was probably the first person to eat meat between two slices of bread. According to legend, he once hosted a 24-hour-long card game. He didn't want his fingers to get greasy from meat. He asked his servant to place some meat between two pieces of bread and hand it to him. This was considered terrible table manners, but it caught on among card players. Sandwiches became common at other informal meals, too.

6. Which sentence is an opinon?

   F John Montagu was the fourth Earl of Sandwich.

   G Montagu once hosted a 24-hour-long card game.

   H People who eat sandwiches during card games have bad manners.

   J Sandwiches became common at other informal meals.

7. Which is the best paraphrase of this passage?

   A John Montagu liked to eat while playing cards. Sometimes the card games lasted 24 hours. He used the bread so his fingers wouldn't become greasy.

   B The sandwich was named after John Montagu, the Earl of Sandwich. Montagu used to host long card games. His servant gave him slices of meat on bread to eat during the card games. At first, this way of eating was thought to be rude, but it soon became popular at informal meals.

   C The sandwich was invented to eat during card games. Some people thought this was rude.

   D John Montagu put meat between bread.

(1) The giraffe and the mouse seem to have nothing in common, aside from both being animals. (2) The mouse is a tiny creature. (3) Most mice never grow to be more than a few inches long. (4) Giraffes, on the other hand, are huge. (5) Some zoos have giraffes. (6) A giraffe's neck alone can be more than six feet long. (7) However, in one way they are just alike. (8) It is their necks that the mouse and giraffe have in common. (9) The necks of both are made up of bones called vertebrae. (10) Though they differ greatly in size, the mouse and the giraffe have the same number of vertebrae in their necks.

8. Which sentence is NOT important to understanding the topic?

   F sentence 1

   G sentence 5

   H sentence 8

   J sentence 10

9. This passage is about

   A all the ways that giraffes and mice are different.

   B all the ways that giraffes and mice are alike.

   C some ways that mice and giraffes are alike and different.

   D the size of mice and giraffes.

> (1) If you are like many people, you probably get in the shower and wash your hair daily. (2) Showering every day uses a lot of water. (3) If you shampoo every day, you may be hurting your hair. (4) Skin doctors say you should skip some days. (5) You should wash your hair gently. (6) First, start with a gentle scalp massage. (7) Then shampoo your hair, but be careful not to rub too hard. (8) All that scrubbing might damage your hair. (9) After that, rinse the shampoo out completely. (10) Finally, use a conditioner. (11) You don't have to buy expensive products that have protein and vitamins added to them. (12) Hair probably cannot be nourished from the outside.

10. Which sentence does NOT support the main idea of the passage?

   F sentence 2

   G sentence 5

   H sentence 8

   J sentence 10

11. When you wash your hair, which of these steps should you do last?

   A Use a conditioner.

   B Rinse the shampoo out.

   C Massage your scalp.

   D Shampoo your hair.

12. According to the passage, what is a possible effect of shampooing every day?

   F You look like most people.

   G Your hair might become damaged.

   H You need to use conditioner.

   J Your hair gets nourished.

13. The writer's style creates an effect of

   A fear.

   B authority.

   C saracsm.

   D anger.

> Marina spoke softly and gently to her mother, "Yes, Mama. Is that better, Mama?" She fluffed her mother's pillows. She gave her mother her medicine. She prepared delicious meals. Her mother could be very demanding. At times, she spoke sharply to her daughter, yet Marina was always kind and never complained. "Poor Mama," she thought. "Her life has shrunk to the size of a room. I should bring flowers to brighten her day."

14. Which traits best describe Marina?

   F demanding and cruel

   G hardworking and careful

   H caring and patient

   J cold and selfish

15. Which style technique does the author use in the passage?

   A short, choppy sentences

   B informal language

   C punctuation for emphasis

   D dialogue

Study the graph. Then circle the letter of the answer to each question.

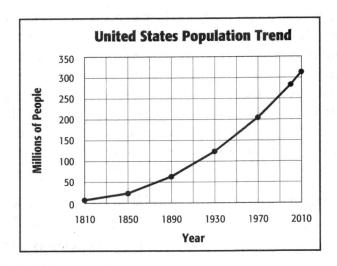

United States Population Trend

16. What does the horizontal axis on the graph show?

 F   number of people

 G   percentage of people

 H   years

 J   miles

17. In what year was the population about 125,000,000?

 A   1850

 B   1930

 C   1970

 D   2010

18. Based on the graph, what do you predict the population trend will be after 2010?

 F   The population will stay the same.

 G   The population will probably grow.

 H   The population will probably shrink.

 J   There isn't enough information to make a prediction.

19. What was the U.S. population in 1970?

 A   about 10 million

 B   about 25 million

 C   about 200 million

 D   about 310 million

Read the passage. Then circle the letter of the answer to each question.

> Paolo has completed his homework assignments on time every week this year. He has earned A's on quizzes and tests. Paolo has made the straight-A honor roll every semester for the past three years.

20. What character traits does Paolo show?

 F   lazy and tired

 G   energetic and artistic

 H   hardworking and studious

 J   ambitious and ruthless

21. What generalization can you make about Paolo?

 A   Paolo never has fun.

 B   Paolo is not interested in grades.

 C   Paolo hates to study.

 D   Paolo takes school seriously.

Pretest continued

Study the index. Then circle the letter of the answer to each question.

Index

Caribbean coast, 612–625

    beaches, 614

    lodging, 620–625

    restaurants, 618–620

    shopping, 618

    sightseeing, 613–617

    sports, 619

    transportation, 612

Caves, 412, 525, 590

Chapala (lake), 79

Chichen Itza (Maya ruins), 275–276

Children

    traveling with, 150–155

    what to do, 155–165

Coba (Maya ruins), 301–302

Dance, 115–118

    festivals of, 21

    flamenco, 313

Dining, 80–120

    (See also **Restaurants**)

---

22. On which page would you find information about lodging?

  F 80–120

  G 275–276

  H 301–302

  J 620–625

23. Which topic is discussed on page 79?

  A beaches

  B transportation

  C Chichen Itza

  D Lake Chapala

Read the passage. Then circle the letter of the answer to each question.

The *Mona Lisa* was the victim of the most famous art heist in history. In 1911 it was stolen from the Louvre in the early morning when no one was looking. The painting was missing for two years. It was a devastating loss to the art world. Thousands of visitors went to the Louvre to see the empty spot where the painting had once hung.

---

24. Which of these statements is an opinion?

  F In 1911 it was stolen from the Louvre in the early morning when no one was looking.

  G The painting was missing for two years.

  H It was a devastating loss to the art world.

  J Thousands of visitors went to the Louvre to see the empty spot where the painting had once hung.

25. Who stole the *Mona Lisa* from the Louvre?

  A one of the security guards

  B one of the visitors who went to see the empty spot

  C a professional art thief

  D not stated

Read the lease agreement. Then circle the letter of the answer to each question.

Lease Agreement

This lease covers the property at 1417 Lee Street, Apartment 10C, in Lake Forest, Indiana. The property is to be used and occupied by Lessee as a residence and for no other purpose from September 1 to August 31.

RENT. Monthly rent of $950.00 shall be paid by Lessee to Lessor. It is due on or before the first day of every month. A penalty of $100 shall be fined by Lessor against Lessee for each and every rent payment more than five (5) business days late.

SECURITY DEPOSIT. On signing the lease, Lessee makes a security deposit of $1,500. The deposit will be returned with one percent (1%) interest if the apartment is in good condition when the lease ends and is not renewed.

---

26. What do you predict will happen if the rent is paid more than 10 business days late?

    F   There is no penalty for late payments.

    G   The security deposit will not be returned.

    H   A $100 fine will be added to the rent payment.

    J   The lease will not be renewed.

27. The property being rented can be used for

    A   a residence and a daycare center.

    B   a residence only.

    C   a daycare center only.

    D   any type of business.

28. When does the Lessee get his or her security deposit back?

    F   when the lease ends and is renewed

    G   when the Lessee pays 1% interest

    H   when the lease ends and is not renewed

    J   when the Lessee signs the lease

29. Who is the Lessee?

    A   the person renting the property

    B   the owner of the property

    C   the bank that holds the mortgage

    D   the person who previously rented the property

30. How much is the required security deposit?

    F $100

    G $950

    H $1,500

    J $1,150

31. As used in the lease, the term *residence* means

    A   person signing a lease.

    B   place to live.

    C   property.

    D   business.

32. On what day is the rent due?

    F   the fifth day of the month

    G   the last day of the month

    H   by August 31

    J   the first day of the month

33. What is the best summary of the last paragraph?

    A   When the lease ends, the Lessee will receive the security deposit plus 1% interest if the apartment is in good condition.

    B   When the lease ends and is not renewed, the landlord will evaluate the condition of the apartment.

    C   The Lessee will get the security deposit back.

    D   The Lessee will clean the apartment.

Read the workplace document from a hospital procedures manual. Then circle the letter of the answer to each question.

SECTION 7: PROTECTION OF LAUNDRY WORKERS

Laundry workers handle a large amount of soiled linen each day. It is the job of the laundry department to return used linen in a clean and safe condition. Failure to do so can cause cross-infection throughout the hospital. Laundry workers also have a right to proper protection at all times.

7.1 Staff who handle used, unwashed linen in the sorting areas should wear protective clothing. This includes waterproof aprons and gloves. However, the use of surgical face masks is not considered necessary.

7.2 Staff should be up-to-date on all vaccinations.

7.3 Any cuts on the skin must be covered with a waterproof bandage.

7.4 Hand-washing and dressing rooms are provided in accordance with current legislation. Workers must wear clean overalls. These are available to staff at each new shift or work period change.

7.5 Staff must be fully trained in all laundry operations, including cleaning and operational procedures.

---

34. Failure to properly clean hospital linen can cause

   F the need to wear protective clothing.

   G cuts on workers' skin.

   H problems with vaccinations.

   J cross-infection throughout the hospital.

35. The author's purpose in these guidelines is to

   A explain current legislation.

   B inform laundry workers about how to stay safe.

   C describe the types of germs in hospital laundries.

   D tell a frightening story.

36. As used in guideline 7.1, *handle* means

   F "the part of an object that is held."

   G "to touch with the hands."

   H "as much as a hand can hold."

   J "easily reached."

37. Which is the main job of laundry workers?

   A to launder staff overalls

   B to be familiar with current legislation

   C to return linen in a clean and safe condition

   D to fully train others in operational procedures

38. When can workers receive clean overalls?

   F on their first day of employment

   G as old overalls get dirty

   H at the end of each shift

   J at the start of each new shift or work period change

39. What should be covered with a waterproof bandage?

   A any burns

   B any cuts on the skin

   C any rashes

   D not stated

40. What is the main idea of this document?

   F Laundry workers must wear clean clothing while they launder linens.

   G Laundering linens is important to prevent cross-infection.

   H It is important for staff to thoroughly clean linens and to protect themselves while doing it.

   J Covering wounds and wearing protective clothing is very important.

Read the workplace document. Then circle the letter of the answer to each question.

SHADY ACRES

Landscaping and Tree Service Application Form

Thank you for your interest in Shady Acres Landscaping, Inc. We'd like to have information to see how your abilities fit our team. Please send your completed form to Lou Santarpo at 1345 High Street, Ceredo, WV 25507.

Name _____   DOB _____

	YES	NO
Do you have a fear of heights?	☐	☐
Can you operate a bucket truck?	☐	☐
Does your driver's license allow you to drive trucks?	☐	☐
Do you own your own truck or other vehicle?	☐	☐
Do you own landscaping equipment?	☐	☐
Are you accustomed to working outdoors?	☐	☐
Are you able to do physically challenging work?	☐	☐
Are you allergic to pollen?	☐	☐
Are you allergic to bee stings?	☐	☐
Do you have any other allergies?	☐	☐

If yes, please explain: _____

Have you done landscaping work in the past?	☐	☐

If so, please explain on the back of this form.

41. When might you need to fill out a form like this?
    A when you place a catalog order by mail
    B when you apply for a job
    C when you apply for a credit card
    D when you request office supplies

42. As used in this form, *operate* means
    F "conduct military activities"
    G "be in effect"
    H "perform surgery"
    J "control the function of"

43. What do the letters DOB stand for?
    A date of birth
    B dog or bird
    C diameter of bark
    D dark or blond

44. Which generalization can you make from the questions on the form?
    F Everyone who owns a truck is wealthy.
    G Landscapers and tree workers should be used to working outdoors.
    H People who fear heights should not mow lawns.
    J People with pollen and bee allergies enjoy landscape work.

Pretest continued

Circle the letter of the word that is spelled correctly and fits in the sentence.

45. You should wait for all the _____ to ripen.

    A peach

    B peachs

    C peaches

    D peachses

46. _____ the first person to arrive.

    F You're

    G Yure

    H Your

    J Yeer

47. I _____ the heavy box into the house.

    A carryed

    B carryeid

    C carryied

    D carried

48. People used to write letters on fancy _____.

    F stationary

    G stationery

    H statonary

    J stationry

49. The _____ of the high school recently retired.

    A principal

    B principle

    C princeple

    D principul

50. Do you know _____ gloves these are?

    F whos

    G who's

    H whoes

    J whose

Circle the letter of the answer to each question.

51. Which word is NOT divided correctly into syllables?

    A mumb / le

    B spi / der

    C rib / bon

    D poo / dle

52. Which word does NOT have a long *u* vowel sound?

    F ruler

    G suit

    H hunger

    J foolish

53. Which contraction is spelled correctly?

    A cant

    B can'

    C can't

    D c'ant

54. Which word fits into both sentences?

    My _____ is running a few minutes fast.

    Can you _____ the baby tomorrow while I work?

    F change

    G watch

    H sign

    J play

55. Which phrase means "the anniversary of our parents"?

    A our parentses anniversary

    B our parent's anniversary

    C our parents anniversary

    D our parents' anniversary

56. Which word has an open first syllable?

    F scribble

    G scallop

    H station

    J stallion

57. Which phrase means "the radio belonging to Hoon"?

   A Hoon's radio

   B Hoons' radio

   C Hoons radio

   D Hoon radio

58. Which word means *less than zero*?

   F prezero

   G nonzero

   H subzero

   J zeroless

59. What is the meaning of the prefix *tri-*?

   A three

   B try

   C two

   D ten

60. Which word does NOT have an *r*-controlled vowel sound?

   F score

   G skirt

   H scarf

   J scruff

61. Which word has the same vowel sound as *frown*?

   A lawn

   B house

   C grow

   D haunt

62. Which word has three syllables?

   F superiority

   G superior

   H supervise

   J supervisor

63. Which word is a compound word?

   A basketball

   B hockey

   C soccer

   D rugby

64. Which is the base word in the word *rearranging*?

   F arranging

   G rearrange

   H arrange

   J rearranging

65. Which contraction is spelled correctly?

   A wouldve

   B wouldv'e

   C wouldve'

   D would've

66. What is one meaning of *reasonable*?

   F below a reason

   G to reason with again

   H not reasoned with

   J able to be reasoned with

67. Which word is a synonym for *anxious*?

   A reluctant

   B delighted

   C worried

   D calm

68. Which word is an antonym for *repair*?

   F return

   G fix

   H build

   J break

69. Which word has a silent letter?

   A wrap

   B wing

   C raft

   D water

70. Which word fits into both sentences?

   I need a _____ to get the campfire going.

   Does this sweater _____ your skirt?

   F match

   G fire

   H log

   J line

This pretest was designed to help you determine which reading skills you need to study. This chart shows which skill is being covered with each test question. Use the key on page 12 to check your answers. Then circle the questions you answered incorrectly and go to the practice pages in this book covering those skills.

Tested Skills	Question Numbers	Practice Pages
Recognize and Recall Details	27, 30, 32	14–17
Understand Stated Concepts	1, 25, 37, 39	22–25
Draw Conclusions	3	30–33
Summarize and Paraphrase	7, 33	38–41
Compare and Contrast	9	46–49
Use Forms	41–44	54–57
Find the Main Idea	4, 40	62–65
Identify Sequence	11, 38	78–81
Use Supporting Evidence	8, 10	86–89
Identify Style Techniques	15	94–97
Make Generalizations	21, 44	102–105
Author's Purpose, Effect, Intention	5, 13, 35	110–113
Read Graphs	16–19	118–121
Predict Outcomes	18, 26	134–137
Identify Cause and Effect	12, 28, 34	142–145
Understand Consumer Materials	26–33	150–153
Recognize Character Traits	14, 20	158–161
Identify Fact and Opinion	6, 24	166–169
Use Indexes	22, 23	174–177
Synonyms/Antonyms	67, 68	37, 45, 84, 92, 141
Context Clues	2, 29, 31, 36, 42, 54, 70	60, 68, 69, 116, 140, 165
Spelling	45–50, 53, 55, 57, 65, 69	21, 28, 44, 52, 61, 85, 100, 109, 117, 124, 125, 148, 156, 157, 172, 181
Phonics/Word Analysis	51, 52, 56, 58–64, 66	20, 21, 28, 29, 36, 44, 52, 53, 60, 68, 84, 92, 93, 100, 101, 108, 116, 124, 140, 148, 149, 156, 164, 172, 173, 180

	KEY		
1.	D	36.	G
2.	F	37.	C
3.	A	38.	J
4.	H	39.	B
5.	D	40.	H
6.	H	41.	B
7.	B	42.	J
8.	G	43.	A
9.	C	44.	G
10.	F	45.	C
11.	A	46.	F
12.	G	47.	D
13.	B	48.	G
14.	H	49.	A
15.	D	50.	J
16.	H	51.	A
17.	B	52.	H
18.	G	53.	C
19.	C	54.	G
20.	H	55.	D
21.	D	56.	H
22.	J	57.	A
23.	D	58.	H
24.	H	59.	A
25.	D	60.	J
26.	H	61.	B
27.	B	62.	H
28.	H	63.	A
29.	A	64.	H
30.	H	65.	D
31.	B	66.	J
32.	J	67.	C
33.	A	68.	J
34.	J	69.	A
35.	B	70.	F

Unit 1

In this unit you will learn how to

You will practice the following workplace skills

You will also learn new words and their meanings and put your reading skills to work in written activities. You will get additional reading practice in *Reading Basics Intermediate 1 Reader*.

Lesson 1.1

Recognize and Recall Details

Every passage has a topic, which is what the passage is about. When you begin to read, identify the topic. Then pay attention to the important details as you read. The important details are those that give information related to the topic.

Some details may be facts. Suppose you are reading about the United States. One important detail to remember is that there are 50 states in the United States. Other details may describe how something looks, sounds, or feels. Suppose you are reading an article about poison ivy. You would want to remember details that describe what this plant looks like.

While reading you might find details that are not relevant to the topic. That is, they are not connected or related to the topic. These details do not help you to understand the topic. Read the example:

> Silver is a precious metal. It is relatively scarce. It is used in jewelry making and to make coins and decorative objects. It is also highly conductive. It is used in electronic conductors and electrical servers. Silver is usually mined as a by-product of other metals. Today South Africa produces about one-third of the world's gold.

In the example above, the topic is silver. The last sentence, which gives a detail about gold, is not relevant.

If you can recognize and recall important details, you will better understand what you read. You may enjoy it more too.

The topic of the passage is glass snakes. Read the passage. Then underline the sentence with details that are NOT relevant.

> Glass snakes are a kind of legless lizard. They live in the United States and Mexico. They grow to be about two feet long. Glass snakes have long tails that break easily. A glass snake uses its tail to trick its enemies. When a glass snake is being chased, it starts to twitch its tail. When the enemy attacks the tail, it breaks off. Then the glass snake gets away. Glass snakes can grow new tails to replace the old ones. Iguanas also lose their tails, but their tails don't always grow back.

Did you underline the last sentence? That sentence gives information about iguanas, not glass snakes, so these details are not relevant to understanding the topic.

Read the passage. Then circle the letter of the answer to each question.

Many people who visit the seashore collect seashells. Some people look for shells with the sea creatures still in them. These shells are likely to be in the best condition. However, creatures that live inside shells can have poisonous stings. Most people just collect empty shells. The best time to find empty shells is after a storm. I like to visit the beach in the morning. Some shell collectors clean and label their shells. Other collectors, like artists, make jewelry and decorations out of the prettiest shells.

1. What is the topic of this passage?

   A   people who collect seashells

   B   different kinds of seashells

   C   things to do at the beach

   D   people who enjoy hobbies

2. According to the passage, what do some artists do with the shells they collect?

   F   They clean and label the shells.

   G   They look for sea creatures still in the shells.

   H   They make jewelry from the shells.

   J   They throw the shells back into the sea.

3. Which detail is NOT important?

   A   Some people look for shells with the sea creatures still in them.

   B   Some shell collectors clean and label their shells.

   C   Most people just collect empty shells.

   D   I like to visit the beach in the morning.

4. When is the best time for a collector to find empty shells?

   F   during a vacation to a waterfall

   G   in the early morning, around sunrise

   H   after a storm

   J   during a lightning storm

5. Which kind of shells are usually in the best condition?

   A   shells that are cleaned and labeled

   B   shells that you collect in the morning

   C   shells that have washed up on the beach

   D   shells with sea creatures inside them

Read each passage. Then follow the instructions.

Molds grow in many places, often when and where you don't want them. Molds can be harmful to people, but some molds are good. Many types of mold grow on food and have a fuzzy appearance. They feed on sugars found in bread, fruit, and other foods. Throw away food that has expired. Unwanted mold can spoil a food's taste. However, mold can actually add to a food's flavor. Certain cheeses need mold to ripen them and give them their distinct taste. Blue cheeses such as Gorgonzola and Roquefort get their distinctive taste and coloring from mold.

Write four details from the passage about molds.

1. _____
2. _____
3. _____
4. _____

Write the sentence that is not relevant to the topic.

5. _____

Have you ever wondered where all the salt in the ocean came from? Scientists have been trying to answer this question for years. No one knows the answer for sure. One theory is that long ago Earth was dry, and there were many rocks that contained salt. The oceans were formed when water vapor in the air cooled and condensed into liquid water. The water washed salt off the rocks and into the oceans as they formed. After a time, the oceans became full of salt. Today every gallon of seawater has about a quarter of a pound of salt in it.

Write four details from the passage about the salt in the ocean.

6. _____
7. _____
8. _____
9. _____

Read the passage. Then circle the letter of the answer to each question.

Many people got rich during the Klondike gold rush. In 1898 the town of Dawson was filled with prospectors. Thousands of people went to Dawson hoping to make their fortunes from gold. A few of them, however, got rich without mining for gold. They set up grocery stores in Dawson. The prospectors had to eat, and most of them cooked over campfires. The prospectors had no choice but to buy from the stores. Dawson grocers sold eggs for $18 a dozen. They sold milk for $3 a can. The miners who went in search of gold were taking a risk. The people who sold groceries to those miners were certain of making their fortunes.

1. Often the title states the topic of a passage. Which is the best title for this passage?
   A Life in the 19th Century
   B Striking It Rich in Dawson
   C Milk and Eggs
   D The Gold Rush

2. Why did prospectors rush to the Klondike in the 19th century?
   F to eat
   G to raise chickens
   H to buy groceries
   J to mine gold

3. Opening a grocery store in the Klondike
   A was very risky.
   B was a sure way to make money.
   C was more risky than mining gold.
   D was doomed for failure.

4. Which of these sentences is an unimportant detail in the passage?
   F Some people set up grocery stores in Dawson.
   G Dawson was filled with prospectors.
   H Most prospectors cooked over campfires.
   J They sold eggs for $18 a dozen.

5. Why did the prospectors buy food from the expensive grocery stores?
   A There was nowhere else to shop.
   B They liked specialty food items.
   C The grocers accepted the prospectors' gold as payment.
   D They were friends with the store owners.

Workplace Skill:
Locate and Recall Details in a Job Description

Details are facts that support the main idea of a passage or text. When you read, it is important to locate the main idea and the supporting details. When reading a job description, look for these main facts first: the job title, salary, and hours. Then read anything that is underlined or in bold print. If you are still interested in the job, read the rest of the description.

Read the job description. Then circle the letter of the answer to each question.

EMPLOYMENT OPPORTUNITY
CITY PARKS DEPARTMENT

Maintenance Worker

Salary: $17.40 per hour, 40 hours per week

The maintenance worker does many different tasks. These include

• mowing and trimming grassy areas.

• clearing weeds and brush.

• maintaining and removing trees.

• maintaining athletic fields and playground areas.

• installing and repairing fences.

Applicants must be able to work as part of a team. Applicants must also be

• experienced in maintaining grounds and driving trucks and other vehicles.

• able to use equipment safely.

• able to do hard manual labor.

This work includes walking, lifting, stooping, and carrying.

Applicants must be at least 18 years old and have a valid driver's license.

Apply to Department of Human Resources, Room 128, City Hall.

1. How many hours per week should the maintenance worker expect to work?

   A 37 hours per week

   B less than 35 hours per week

   C less than 40 hours per week

   D 40 hours per week

2. What is one important detail from the job description that an applicant should know?

   F You must have experience in tree removal.

   G You must be 18 years old and have a driver's license.

   H You must have 20/20 vision.

   J You will be working on your own and without supervision.

Write for Work

Read the job description on page 18. In a notebook, write a paragraph explaining why you do or do not think being a maintenance worker is a good job for you. Use details from the job description to support your opinion.

 Reading Extension

Turn to "The Man-Eaters of Tsavo" on page 1 of *Reading Basics Intermediate 1 Reader*. After you have read and/or listened to the article, answer the questions below.

Circle the letter of the answer to each question.

1. The "man-eaters of Tsavo" lived in
   A Chicago.
   B east Africa.
   C the East Indies.
   D Great Britain.

2. Many of the lions' victims were
   F railroad workers.
   G campers.
   H goats.
   J hunters.

3. What did Colonel Patterson use to kill the lions?
   A poisoned meat
   B a machete
   C a gun
   D a snare

4. How many lions made up the "man-eaters of Tsavo"?
   F one
   G two
   H too many to count
   J No one knows for sure.

5. Because they were so scared, many of the workers
   A ran away.
   B carried rifles.
   C refused to sleep.
   D played loud music.

6. Where can you see the "man-eaters of tsavo" today?
   F at a railroad station in east Africa
   G outside the New York Public Library
   H in the Chicago Field Museum
   J near the Tsavo River

Write the answer to each question.

7. What are two details that describe the first dead lion?

_____

_____

8. Reread paragraphs 3 and 4. What are two facts about Colonel Patterson?

_____

_____

Explore Words

LONG VOWELS

The letters *a, e, i, o,* and *u* are vowels. Every vowel has a short sound and a long sound. You can hear the short vowel sounds in these words: *glad, help, fish, stop,* and *sum.* You can hear the long vowel sounds in these words: *stale, Pete, smile, home, rule,* and *cube.*

Complete each sentence with the word that has a long vowel sound. Write the new sentence on the line. The first item has been done for you.

1. (Liz, Steve) got a good job.

   Steve got a good job.

2. Mr. Garcia got a new (clock, bike).

   _____

3. Akil made a table from (wood, pine).

   _____

4. Will you please pass the (cake, dip)?

   _____

5. Lomasi thinks my friend is (fun, cute).

   _____

6. I will give her his (phone, cell) number.

   _____

CONSONANT BLENDS

The consonants *s, l, r,* and *n* can blend with other consonants. A consonant blend can come at the beginning or at the end of a word. A consonant blend can consist of two or three letters. The following words have two-letter consonant blends: *grab, small, pest, bank,* and *belt.* These words have three-letter blends: *spring, strike,* and *split.* When you see a consonant blend, say the sound of each consonant in the blend.

Read each sentence. Then complete each word with one of the consonant blends in parentheses. Make sure the word fits the meaning of the sentence. The first item has been done for you.

1. Carla has a new __*gr*__een dress for the party. (bl, sl, gr)

2. My son's teacher is very _____ict about classroom behavior. (spr, scr, str)

3. Who do you thi_____ will win the basketball game? (sk, nk, st)

4. I need to _____ay the plants twice a week. (sm, str, spr)

5. I have about $500 in my ba_____ account. (sk, nk, st)

6. José finished fir_____ in the cross-country race. (sk, nk, st)

7. I have not _____ept in five days. (sm, pr, sl)

COMPOUND WORDS

A compound word is a word made from two words. For example: *springtime* is a compound word. It is made from the words *spring* and *time*.

Read each word. Then write the letter C on the line if the word is a compound word.

1. blueberry _____

2. worthwhile _____

3. afternoon _____

4. splinter _____

5. backyard _____

6. sparrow _____

7. airport _____

8. magnet _____

9. earthquake _____

SPELLING: POSSESSIVES

Read the words *child's coat*. Notice the *'s* at the end of the word *child's*. It is used to show possession. Possessive words show that something belongs to a person or thing.

Read the phrases. Use *'s* to write possessive words. The first item has been done for you.

1. the restaurant that belongs to Dave _*Dave's restaurant*_

2. the food that the baby gets _____

3. the toy that was given to Youko _____

4. the ribbons that belong to my niece _____

ACADEMIC VOCABULARY

Knowing these high-frequency words will help you in many school subjects.

topic   the subject of a passage, article, or book

details   facts and descriptions that give information

recall   to remember

theory   an idea about how or why something happens

passage   a short piece of writing

Complete the sentences below using one of the words above.

1. The detective has a _____ about who is breaking into cars.

2. I do not _____ meeting her before today.

3. The librarian can help you find books on any _____.

4. I need to find out more _____ about the job offer.

5. When you have time, read this _____.

Lesson 1.2

Understand Stated Concepts

Every passage contains information. Often important concepts, or facts and ideas, are stated directly. Make sure to pay attention to the stated concepts. Then you will better understand what you read. Note that when answering questions about a concept stated in a passage, the answer may not appear exactly as it is stated in the passage. Read the example:

> Amelia was born in New York City—and she's never left. She loves her city, especially the noise and the people, but she wants to travel to somewhere new.

Where has Amelia lived all her life? New York City. The passage doesn't state that directly. It states that she was born there and never left, but it means the same thing.

It's often a good idea to underline or highlight important concepts as you read. This is especially true if you are reading something long or complicated. You can also make notes in the margin or in a notebook. This will help you better understand and remember important facts.

There may be times when you are asked a question and the answer is not given in the passage you have read. If this happens, reread the passage carefully. If you are certain that the answer is not in the passage, choose *not stated*.

Read the passage. Then answer the question by underlining the sentence where you found the answer.

(1) The gas in your stove has probably traveled a long distance. (2) Most natural gas is trapped below Earth's surface. (3) Holes are drilled through the ground to get to this gas. (4) Then the gas is pumped through huge pipelines. (5) Pipes can be as wide as 60 inches across. (6) The gas is pumped at high pressure. (7) A network of pipes covers the country. (8) The gas arrives in pipes at the gas company. (9) From there it is sent out to homes through more pipes. (10) Someone living in New York might be getting gas that has come all the way from Texas, more than 1,500 miles away.

Where does natural gas come from?

Did you underline sentence 2? It says, "Most natural gas is trapped below Earth's surface." This stated concept is important to remember because it will help you to better understand the rest of the passage.

Read the passage. Then read each sentence that follows. If the information is stated in the passage, write *stated*. If it is not stated, write *not stated*.

> When Harvard College opened in the 17th century, it was very different from today's Harvard University. Only male students were allowed to attend. To be admitted as a student, an applicant had to be able to read, write, and speak in Latin. The school was small and had few resources. The only heat came from fireplaces, and the school's few students read and studied by candlelight.

1. Harvard College was founded in 1636. _____

2. Students at Harvard in the 17th century studied by candlelight. _____

3. Latin is a very difficult language to learn. _____

Read the passage. Then circle the letter of the answer to each question.

> Hummingbirds are very good fliers. Flying backwards is one trick that they perform easily. Most other birds land or fly to a higher level gradually, but not the hummingbird! It can drop straight down or fly straight up, and it's the only bird that can hover in midair. That is why this bird is often compared to a helicopter. The hummingbird has a strong set of wings. Its wings beat so quickly that they make a whirring noise. This is what gives the bird the "hum" for which it is named.

4. What is a hummingbird compared to in this passage?

   A an airplane

   B a helicopter

   C a rocket

   D a parachute

5. According to the passage, in what way is a hummingbird different from other birds?

   F It can hover in midair.

   G It cannot move around on land.

   H It cannot swim.

   J It beats its wings 70 times per second.

6. A hummingbird's name refers to

   A the whirring noise its wings make.

   B the song it sings when it flies.

   C the shape of its wings.

   D the noise a helicopter makes.

7. Which information is not stated in the passage?

   F Hummingbirds are good fliers.

   G Hummingbirds have strong wings.

   H Its wings make a whirring noise.

   J Hummingbirds live only a few years.

Read each passage. Then answer the questions.

A bolt of lightning is a great spark caused by an electric current. Water droplets in thunderclouds are charged with electricity. Different clouds have different charges. Opposite charges attract each other. When they meet, they form a lightning bolt. It is like a very large spark. Lightning can take place within one cloud or between a cloud and Earth. A bolt of lightning can kill a person or start a fire.

1. What is lightning?

_____

2. Why is lightning considered to be dangerous?

_____

3. List two places where lightning can occur.

_____

We always have tears in our eyes, even when we aren't crying. Eyes need tears at all times. Without tears, we would go blind. Tears keep eyes moist and help keep out dust. Tears come from glands that are behind the upper eyelids. They bathe the eyes and then flow out through tear ducts. Tear ducts are drains in the corners of the eyes nearest the nose. They are hidden inside the lower eyelid. When we cry, we let out too many tears for the ducts to handle—so they overflow.

4. Why do you need tears?

_____

5. Where do tears come from?

_____

6. What happens when we cry?

_____

7. What are tear ducts?

_____

Read the passage. Then circle the letter of the answer to each question.

Whales, porpoises, and dolphins all live in the ocean, but they cannot breathe underwater. Like elephants, tigers, and many other land animals, they are mammals. Mammals give birth to live babies instead of laying eggs. Mammals also grow hair and breathe air. Sea mammals don't get oxygen from water, as fish do. They have well-developed lungs and can hold their breath for a long time. It isn't just for fun that they dive and surface. They have to come out of the water to breathe air.

1. Which of the following concepts was stated?

    A   People are mammals.

    B   Otters and seals are sea mammals.

    C   Mammals cannot breathe underwater.

    D   People enjoy watching dolphins.

2. What major difference between fish and sea mammals was stated in this passage?

    F   Fish get oxygen from the water, but sea mammals do not.

    G   Whales are much bigger than any fish.

    H   Whales like to play on the surface of the water, but fish do not.

    J   Dolphins stay in deep water, but some fish can be found in shallow water.

3. Why do sea mammals dive and surface?

    A   to grow hair

    B   to breathe air

    C   to give birth to babies

    D   to look like fish

4. According to the statements in the passage, sea mammals

    F   are as big as elephants.

    G   have well-developed lungs.

    H   can breath underwater.

    J   lay eggs like fish and birds.

5. Listed below are important facts about mammals. Which one is stated in this passage?

    A   Mammals are warm-blooded animals.

    B   Mammals are one of six main classes of animals.

    C   Mammals give birth to live babies.

    D   Mammals live in every habitat on Earth.

Workplace Skill: Find Stated Concepts in a Mission Statement

A mission statement is a brief description of a company's fundamental purpose and focus. It is meant both for those in the organization and the general public. In a mission statement, a writer states the concepts that are most important to the company. Headings and titles are often used to draw attention to the main concepts.

Read the mission statement. Then circle the letter of the answer to each question.

GZ Mattress Company Mission Statement

Our Goal: We strive to be the top manufacturer of mattresses in the world. In order to meet this goal, we will ensure that our products and designs are superior to all others.

Our Pledge: We promise to provide high-quality, cost-effective mattresses to improve the quality of our customers' sleep.

Our Professionalism: Our standards include a commitment to courtesy, service, and respect. We always put our customers first. We expect all employees to adhere to these standards. We follow these standards when working with each other and with people outside our company.

1. What is GZ Mattress Company's main goal?

   A   to produce and sell the least expensive mattresses in the world

   B   to produce the most comfortable mattresses in the United States

   C   to be the top manufacturer of mattresses in the world

   D   to make sure employees adhere to their standards

2. What heading helps you find the section on the company's standards?

   F   Our Goal

   G   Our Pledge

   H   Our Professionalism

   J   GZ Mattress Company Mission Statement

3. What idea is NOT directly stated in the mission statement?

   A   Customers can request a copy of the company's mission statement.

   B   The company wants its employees to always put the customer first.

   C   The company is concerned about improving customers' sleep.

   D   Employees should follow the standards with each other and the public.

4. Which is NOT a standard of GZ Matress Company?

   F   commitment to courtesy

   G   commitment to quality

   H   commitment to service

   J   commitment to respect

Write for Work

Imagine you are starting a new business. It could be opening a bicycle shop or selling homemade cookies. In a notebook, write one statement about the goal of your new company. Write one statement about how you will reach your goal. Write another statement about your company's standards.

 Reading Extension

Turn to "Doctors (and Nurses) Without Borders" on page 10 of *Reading Basics Intermediate 1 Reader*. After you have read and/or listened to the article, answer the questions below.

Circle the letter of the answer to each question.

1. The people who work for Doctors Without Borders are all

   A emergency-room doctors.

   B volunteers.

   C refugees.

   D from France.

2. What was Lightfine's job before she joined Doctors Without Borders?

   F emergency-room nurse

   G art teacher

   H child care worker

   J not stated

3. Which word best describes the conditions in which Lightfine lived when she was in Doctors Without Borders?

   A cozy

   B rough

   C comfortable

   D plush

4. When was Doctors Without Borders started?

   F the 1970s

   G the 1980s

   H 1992

   J eight years ago

Write the answer to each question.

5. How did Lightfine's patients feel about her?

   _____

   _____

6. Name two details about Lightfine's house in Nicaragua.

   _____

   _____

Explore Words

CONSONANT BLENDS

When the letter pairs *sh* and *th* come together, they stand for one sound. You can hear these sounds at the beginning of *shine* and *think*. The letter pair *sh* can blend with the letter *r*. You can hear this consonant blend at the beginning of *shrink*. The letter pair *th* can also blend with the letter *r*. You can hear this blend at the beginning of *three*.

Write *shr* or *thr* to make a word in each sentence.

1. Jackson _____ew the ball to me.

2. Make sure to _____ed your old checks.

3. Hot water can _____ink that shirt.

4. I need some _____ead to mend this.

SUFFIX *-able*

A suffix is a word part added to the end of a word. A suffix changes the meaning of the word. For example, the suffix *-able* means "able to be." The meaning of the word *like* changes when you add *-able* to the end. *Likeable* means "able to be liked."

Read each word. Then form a new word by adding the suffix *-able*. Write the new word followed by its meaning.

1. tax _____ _____

2. comfort _____ _____

3. depend _____ _____

4. refund _____ _____

SPELLING: CONTRACTIONS

A contraction is a short way to write two words. *Isn't* is a contraction. It is a shorter way to write the words *is not*. Every contraction has an apostrophe ('). It takes the place of the missing letters. In *isn't*, the apostrophe takes the place of the letter *o* in *not*.

Write the contraction for each pair of words on the line. Choose from the list in the box.

didn't	wouldn't	aren't	don't	shouldn't	couldn't

1. do not _____

2. did not _____

3. should not _____

4. would not _____

5. could not _____

6. are not _____

A syllable is a word part that has one vowel sound. Every word has one or more syllables. For example, the words *rap* and *up* each have one syllable. It is a closed syllable. It has one vowel and ends with one or more consonants. The word *motel* has two syllables. The first syllable is *mo*. It is an open syllable. Open syllables usually have long vowel sounds. The second syllable is *tel*. This syllable is a closed syllable. Closed syllables usually have short vowel sounds. Knowing how to pronounce different types of syllables will help you read unfamiliar words.

Put the syllables together and write the word they form. Then circle any closed syllables. Underline any open syllables twice. The first item has been done for you.

1. bo   gus   _bo gus_

2. la   tex   _____

3. ex   act   _____

4. ho   tel   _____

5. cab   in   _____

6. be   gin   _____

7. mu   sic   _____

8. rob   in   _____

9. ti   ger   _____

10. pock   et   _____

11. drag   on   _____

12. tu   lip   _____

Knowing these high-frequency words will help you in many school subjects.

stated   said in speech or writing

concept   an idea

directly   in a clear way

margin   the blank space at the edge of a printed page

notes   written reminders

Complete the sentences below using one of the words above.

1. Don't talk behind my back. Tell me _____ what you think of me.

2. The article _____ that there was a water shortage.

3. Someone already wrote in the _____ of my book.

4. What is your _____ of hard work?

5. My _____ help me when I study for tests.

Lesson 1.3

Draw Conclusions

A conclusion is an idea you form based on other ideas. You hear or read different facts about a topic. You may already know information about the topic. When you combine new facts with what you already know, you can draw a conclusion. Drawing a conclusion means putting together information:

new facts about a topic + personal knowledge about a topic = conclusion about a topic

Your conclusion must make sense. All the facts you have must fit with your conclusion. If they do, it is a valid conclusion. A conclusion that does not make sense is not a valid conclusion. Read the example:

> Fish take oxygen from water. Whales are different from fish. Whales take oxygen from air. Salmon, tuna, and cod are part of the fish family.

You read that fish take oxygen from water and that whales take oxygen from air. You also read that salmon, tuna, and cod are part of the fish family. You can draw the valid conclusion that they take oxygen from water. If you concluded that salmon take oxygen from air, it would be invalid. Read the example:

> There are more than 2,000 different kinds of gemstones. Gem-quality diamonds are the most prized. They are frequently used in jewelry and can be very valuable.

You might conclude that all gemstones are very valuable, but this would not be valid. The example names only one type of valuable stone, diamond. This is not enough information from which to draw a conclusion.

Read the passage. Then draw a conclusion.

> The blue moonwort bores through ice. Believe it or not, the blue moonwort is a plant that lives in the Swiss Alps, where it is very cold. The moonwort is buried by snow all winter. In spring, it sprouts buds. Some people think that the buds give off a little heat, which softens the ice. Then, as the moonwort stem pushes up, the flower cracks through the top layer of ice.

Use what you read and what you know to draw a conclusion. You probably know that most flowers grow in warm weather. You can conclude that *the blue moonwort can live in colder areas than most flowers*. The facts support this conclusion. It is valid.

Suppose you conclude that *the blue moonwort is a beautiful flower*. It may be true, but it is not supported by evidence in the passage. That makes your conclusion invalid.

Read each passage. Then circle the letter of the answer to each question.

Ibexes are wild mountain goats that live in the Alps. They also live in the mountains of Asia. Ibexes are able to climb slopes that are nearly straight up and down. Although they are large animals, ibexes are good jumpers. These goats are sure-footed and can easily leap from rock to rock. They can leap several yards upward and forward from a standing position.

1. From these facts, you can conclude that
   A ibexes are clumsy and stupid.
   B ibexes do not understand how high up they are.
   C ibexes have adapted to live in mountains.
   D ibexes would make good farm animals.

Some African people were making cloth from tree bark about 5,000 years ago. Native Americans used tree bark to make cloth as well. Both groups used the same process that began with soaking the bark in water. Then they put wet strips of bark together and pounded them with stones. The pounding caused fibers to shake out of the bark and stick together in a process called *felting*. Once dry, the fibers were ready to be shaped into clothing.

2. From these facts, you can conclude that
   F Africans taught Native Americans to make bark cloth.
   G Native Americans once lived in Africa.
   H clothing made from bark was uncomfortable.
   J Native American and African peoples came up with the same way of working with the same material.

Read the passage. Then read the conclusion based on the passage. If the conclusion is supported by the facts, write *valid*. If it is not, write a new conclusion.

The Gila (HE-luh) monster lives in the deserts of Mexico. It also lives in the southwestern United States. It is one of only two lizards that are venomous. When it bites, it locks its jaws and hangs on tight. Then its poison seeps into its victim.

Conclusion: The Gila monster preys on other desert animals.

3. _____

Read each passage. Then write a valid conclusion for each passage.

Birds have very light bones. Like airplanes, they use large amounts of energy. Their bodies release the energy stored in food quickly and well. This helps them stay lightweight. Birds have powerful flight muscles, which are attached to a large breastbone. They also have strong, light feathers. These feathers have many rows of barbs that lock together to make them sturdy and firm.

1. _____

_____

_____

Birds do not know how to fly at birth, even though flying is natural for them. As a baby bird grows, it becomes restless. It starts stretching its wings. It walks around the nest and tests its wings. Some people think that the parent bird helps the baby get strong. It holds food at a distance. Then the baby bird must struggle across the nest to get it. One day, the baby hops over the edge of the nest with its wings spread out. The parents fly off the branch, and the baby follows, flapping its wings furiously. The young bird's skill quickly improves.

2. _____

_____

_____

Most birds do not have to flap their wings constantly to remain in the air. If they did, they would soon be worn out. Instead, the shape of their wings provides lift. The upper surface of the wing is rounded, so air has farther to go over than under the wing. Air above the wing moves faster; this difference creates a higher air pressure under the wing. This is called lift. The larger the wing, the greater the lift. Some big birds soar and glide for a long time without flapping their wings.

3. _____

_____

_____

Read the passage. Then circle the letter of the answer to each question.

An igloo is a type of Inuit ice house. It is strong and weatherproof, and it can be built quickly. First a trench is cut in the snow, and blocks of hard snow are cut from the walls of the trench. Each block is shaped to lean inward when set in place. The blocks are laid in circular rows, one on top of another. Each ring is smaller around than the ring below. At last a small hole is left at the top. A wedge-shaped block is set into the top hole. Then the builder fills cracks with soft snow. After a few days, the inside melts and then refreezes. The igloo is soon transformed into a dome of ice.

1. What can you conclude from the description of the blocks and their placement?
   - **A** The blocks get larger as the igloo goes up.
   - **B** The blocks are perfectly square.
   - **C** An igloo is not a safe house to live in.
   - **D** An igloo is smaller at the top than it is at the bottom.

2. What can you conclude from the last two sentences of the passage?
   - **F** The people in the igloo are cold at night.
   - **G** The ice shell inside the igloo makes it stronger.
   - **H** People who live in an igloo will soon freeze.
   - **J** The melted snow makes the space inside an igloo larger.

3. What can you conclude from the entire passage?
   - **A** Igloos are dangerous houses to build.
   - **B** People can build igloos wherever they live.
   - **C** Igloos are carefully designed and built.
   - **D** Igloos are the strongest houses in the world.

4. Which is NOT a valid conclusion?
   - **F** No more than five people can fit in an igloo.
   - **G** An igloo has a rounded top.
   - **H** An igloo could not be built in a hot climate.
   - **J** An igloo provides protection against the weather.

5. What can you conclude about why the builder fills cracks with soft snow?
   - **A** The builder wants to make the igloo look smoother.
   - **B** The builder wants to keep cold air from entering the igloo.
   - **C** The builder wants to help the igloo freeze.
   - **D** The builder wants to see if it will melt.

Workplace Skill: Draw Conclusions from a Business Ad

Business ads are persuasive messages that try to convince people to buy or use something. Look for persuasive words like *best, must,* and *everyone.* When readers combine information from a text with their own knowledge, they draw conclusions. To be able to draw valid conclusions, pay close attention to what you read.

Read the business ad. Then circle the letter of the answer to each question.

Try Our Summer Menu!

Salvatore's is cooking what's fresh NOW!
Come try our new summer menu. We use only locally grown,
100% organic vegetables.

Take advantage of our farm-fresh specials!
Three-course, fixed-price dinners only $14.99!
($10.99 if you are seated before 6:00 P.M., Monday through Thursday)

Guaranteed freshest ingredients!
Everyone will agree that our dinners are the best!

We're so sure that our ingredients are the freshest that we offer this incredible guarantee:
If you're not satisfied, Salvatore's will invite you to come back—ON US! We aim to please!

1. What is the purpose of this ad?
   A to take part in a celebration
   B to get rid of food that is stale
   C to offer free meals
   D to attract people to the restaurant

2. Salvatore's offers a reduced-price, three-course dinner to people who
   F are older than 65.
   G are willing to have an early dinner.
   H are vegetarians.
   J are farmers.

3. The main point of the ad is that diners should eat at Salvatore's because it has
   A the best menu selection.
   B prime steaks.
   C fresh, organic food.
   D a convenient location.

4. What can you conclude from this ad?
   F The menu will change again in the fall.
   G The menu is the same year-round.
   H Salvatore grows his own vegetables.
   J There is no meat on the menu.

Write for Work

Think of a product to sell or a service you would like to provide. In a notebook, write an ad that you could place in your local paper. Remember to highlight what is special about your product or service. Use persuasive words to convince people to buy your product or service.

 ## Reading Extension

Turn to "The Truth about the Tasaday" on page 18 of *Reading Basics Intermediate 1 Reader*. After you have read and/or listened to the article, answer the questions below.

Circle the letter of the answer to each question.

1. From the article, you can conclude that the Tasaday
   - **A** didn't understand the modern world.
   - **B** didn't know they were part of a hoax.
   - **C** were a real Stone Age tribe.
   - **D** made some money from taking part in the hoax.

2. What can you conclude about the people from *National Geographic*?
   - **F** They were probably in on the hoax with Elizalde.
   - **G** They probably felt angry and foolish about being tricked.
   - **H** They took away the Tasaday's garbage.
   - **J** They gave rice and tobacco to the Tasaday.

3. Reread paragraph 7. From this paragraph, you can conclude that Elizalde
   - **A** wanted everyone to have access to the Tasaday.
   - **B** felt it was important to protect the Tasaday from the outside world.
   - **C** didn't care very much about the Tasaday.
   - **D** wanted to modernize the Tasaday.

4. Reread paragraph 10. What can you conclude about why Elizalde disappeared?
   - **F** He was afraid he would be found to be a fraud.
   - **G** He was killed by the old government.
   - **H** He was afraid the Tasaday would no longer be safe.
   - **J** He had found another tribe to study.

Write the answer to each question.

5. Reread paragraph 9. What can you conclude about most people's belief in the Tasaday?

_____

_____

6. Reread paragraph 17. What can you conclude about the existence of Stone Age tribes?

_____

_____

Explore Words

HARD AND SOFT c

The letter *c* has different sounds. In the words *cave* and *cotton*, the letter *c* has a hard sound. Hard *c* has the same sound as the letter *k*. When the letter *c* is followed by a consonant or the vowel *a* or *o*, it usually has a hard sound. In the words *city* and *celebrate*, the letter *c* has a soft sound. A soft *c* has the same sound as the letter *s*. When the letter *c* is followed by the vowel *e* or *i*, it usually has a soft sound.

Say each word. Then write *hard* or *soft* to show the sound of *c*.

1. cookies _____

2. celery _____

3. class _____

4. cent _____

5. calendar _____

6. cartoon _____

SYLLABLES

A syllable is a word part that has one vowel sound. Every word has one or more syllables. The word *go* has one syllable. It is an open syllable. The word *refine* has two syllables. The first syllable is *re*. It is an open syllable. The second syllable is *fine*. *Fine* ends with a vowel-consonant-*e*. It is a silent *e* syllable. Silent *e* syllables and open syllables usually have long vowel sounds.

Put the two syllables together and write the word they form. Then circle open syllables in the word. Underline any silent *e* syllable twice. The first item has been done for you.

1. fe   male   ___(fe)male___

2. bu   tane   _____

3. in   side   _____

4. hu   mane   _____

5. un   made   _____

6. ba   sis   _____

PREFIXES *sub-*, *in-*

A prefix is a word part that can be added to the beginning of a word. Prefixes change the meanings of words. *Sub-* is a prefix that means "less" or "below." The word *subfreezing* means "below freezing." *In-* is a prefix that can mean "not." *Intolerant* means "not tolerant."

Read each word. Then form a new word by adding the prefix *sub-* or *in-*. Write the word on the line.

1. basement _____

2. experienced _____

3. standard _____

4. complete _____

Synonyms are words that have the same, or almost the same, meanings. For example, *scared* and *frightened* are synonyms.

Match the underlined word in each sentence with a synonym from the box. Write the synonym on the line.

ached	kettle	carpet	difficult
worried	careless	excited	book

1. Kateri was <u>anxious</u> about her answers. _____

2. His muscles <u>hurt</u> after lifting heavy boxes all day. _____

3. It is not <u>hard</u> to pronounce my Korean name. _____

4. Salim scrubbed the stain from the <u>rug</u>. _____

5. She put the <u>teapot</u> on the stove. _____

6. She was <u>sloppy</u> and spilled paint on the floor. _____

7. They were <u>thrilled</u> about their upcoming vacation. _____

8. He finished reading his <u>novel</u> before his train ride ended. _____

ACADEMIC VOCABULARY

Knowing these high-frequency words will help you in many school subjects.

evidence	written statements or facts
conclude	to make a decision or judgment after considering information
valid	based on truth or logic
frequently	very often
supported	backed up

Complete the sentences below using one of the words above.

1. Sanjit _____ comes to visit on Sunday afternoons.

2. The jury will probably _____ that he is guilty.

3. Do you have a _____ reason for calling me so late?

4. The facts _____ the witness's story.

5. Review the _____ before you jump to conclusions.

Lesson 1.4

Summarize and Paraphrase

When you read, you may find that you need to summarize or paraphrase the information. You may need to tell someone else what you have read. You may also want to retell it to yourself in order to remember it or to reinforce your understanding.

A good way to understand a passage is to summarize it. A summary should be much shorter than the original passage. A summary gives only the main idea and most important details. You should exclude unimportant details from a summary.

You can also paraphrase by restating something in your own words and including details. A paraphrase can use simpler words than the original, but it may be about the same length. When you summarize or paraphrase, be sure to include the most important ideas. Read the example:

> A scorpion's stinger can be deadly to insects or spiders. Most scorpions don't have enough poison to harm humans. Their sting may hurt, but it is not life threatening.

A good summary of this passage is, *Most scorpions' stingers do not have enough poison to be life threatening to humans.* A good paraphrase is, *A scorpion's poisonous stinger can kill insects and spiders. If a scorpion stings a human, it will hurt, but it won't be life threatening. Scorpions do not usually have enough venom in their stingers to seriously harm humans.*

Read the passage. Then answer the question.

> If you live next to a dog pound, you won't get much sleep. The dogs bark a lot. You could live next to 100,000 rabbits and never hear them. Some people think that rabbits don't have voices. In fact, rabbits have the ability to make a screaming sound when frightened. However, the screaming sound is rarely heard. Their main defense from other animals is staying still in order to hide.

Which example is a summary and which example is a paraphrase?

Example 1 Although they seem silent, rabbits do have voices. They can scream, but they usually stay quiet when they need to protect themselves.

Example 2 Dogs make plenty of noise when they bark. Rabbits seem to have no voice. In fact, rabbits can scream, but they rarely do. Rabbits prefer to stay silent and remain still in order to hide from other animals.

Example 1 is a summary. It includes the main idea and only the most important details. Example 2 is a paraphrase. It restates the passage and includes many details.

Read each passage. Then circle the letter of the answer to each question.

In Japan, a two-room home can be turned into four rooms in just a few minutes. Many Japanese homes have movable walls. They are not like walls that are in American houses. Instead of using plaster walls, the Japanese use screens to divide rooms. These screens are lightweight and easy to move. As a result, the house can be changed to fit almost any occasion.

---

1. Which of these statements best summarizes the passage?

   A Japanese homes are different from other homes because of their small size and moving parts.

   B Japanese homes generally have only two rooms.

   C The Japanese use lightweight screens as walls, making it easy to change a home's space.

   D Americans use plaster for walls, while the Japanese use lightweight, easy-to-move screens.

Paprika is a spice. It is a red powder ground from the dried pods of chili peppers. Some people think that paprika has no flavor. They think it is used only to add color to food. Paprika does have flavor. It can be warm and slightly sweet. People often don't think of paprika as a source of vitamins because they usually eat small amounts of the spice. In fact, paprika has vitamins A and C. However, people would have to eat a large amount of paprika to equal the amount of vitamin C found in an orange or a grapefruit.

---

2. Which of these statements best summarizes the passage?

   F Because paprika has little flavor, it is used in food mostly for its color and its vitamin content.

   G Paprika is a spice useful for adding color, flavor, and vitamins A and C to foods.

   H Paprika is a better source of vitamins than oranges or grapefruit.

   J Paprika is a spice that is bright red and is powdered.

3. Which of these statements is a good paraphrase of the last two sentences of the passage?

   A In order to get the same amount of vitamin C from paprika that is in an orange or a grapefruit, people would have to eat a lot of paprika.

   B Paprika has more vitamin C than citrus fruits.

   C Citrus fruits contain less vitamin C than paprika, but people eat them more often than they eat paprika.

   D Oranges and grapefruits have more vitamin C than paprika because people eat citrus fruits in larger amounts.

Read the passage and write a summary. The summary should be no more than two sentences. Then write a paraphrase of the passage. Remember to use your own words when you paraphrase.

Inside each of your ears is a tiny, thin flap of skin. It is your eardrum. Behind the eardrum are three tiny bones connected to a canal full of fluid. When sound waves hit your ear, they make your eardrum vibrate. This drumming, in turn, sets the three tiny bones in motion. Finally, all this motion causes the fluid in the canal to vibrate. This stimulates nearby nerve cells that are connected to the brain. What the ear does is translate sound into vibrations. The vibrations are then changed into nerve impulses. These impulses give a message to the brain.

Summary

_____

_____

_____

_____

Paraphrase

_____

_____

_____

_____

_____

_____

_____

_____

_____

_____

_____

Read each item. Then circle the letter of the answer to each question.

1. Sailors have traditionally believed that dolphins bring good luck and should not be harmed.

   Which of the following is a good paraphrase for this sentence?

   A If dolphins swim around a ship at sea, it will have good luck on its voyage.

   B Some creatures are considered lucky.

   C Sailors protect dolphins because they believe dolphins bring good luck.

   D People believe dolphins are able to predict the weather.

2. Some old jobs have been given new job titles. Ministers are clergy, not clergymen. Firemen are firefighters. Why were the names changed? Women now fill many of these jobs. In the past, only men held them.

   Which of the following is a good summary for this passage?

   F Some job titles are changing because women as well as men now hold the jobs.

   G Women now hold jobs that were once held only by men.

   H Clergy and firefighters may be either men or women.

   J Job titles change, but this doesn't mean that the job itself has changed.

3. The only land mammals native to New Zealand are bats. The first humans moved there around A.D. 1000.

   Which of the following is a good paraphrase for these sentences?

   A There was no life in New Zealand until bats moved there.

   B Bats were the only land mammals living in New Zealand until humans arrived around A.D. 1,000.

   C Humans and bats live together in New Zealand.

   D Until humans moved there, New Zealand had many land mammals but no bats.

4. What is a main difference between summaries and paraphrases?

   F A summary is not in your own words, but a paraphrase is.

   G A paraphrase includes more details than a summary.

   H A paraphrase is a copy, but a summary is in your own words.

   J A summary includes details, but a paraphrase does not.

5. A summary can best be defined as

   A a restatement of a passage in your own words.

   B the main idea and the most important details of a passage.

   C a restatement of text that includes details.

   D the main idea of a passage, stated in your own words.

6. A paraphrase can best be defined as

   F a restatement of a passage in your own words.

   G the main idea of a passage plus one or two details.

   H a restatement of text that does not include details.

   J the main idea of a passage, stated in your own words.

Workplace Skill: Summarize and Paraphrase an Article

It is important that you understand information you read in workplace documents. Try putting the ideas into your own words. You can summarize by recalling the most important ideas. You can also paraphrase by recalling the main ideas and the details.

Read the article. Then circle the letter of the answer to each question.

The GED® Testing Service

A high-school diploma is very important. You usually need one before you can apply for a job or for college. When someone passes a GED test, they earn a GED credential. This is awarded by your state department of education and is accepted as equal to a high-school diploma. With it, you have a better chance of getting the job you want.

The letters *GED* stand for *General Educational Development*. The GED test is also called the High School Equivalency Test. There are more than 3,400 testing centers in the United States and Canada. Costs differ from state to state. The GED test fee is different depending on where you take the test. You will have to check with the test center nearest you for fee information. You must meet age and residency requirements. A residency requirement means you must live in a place for a certain period of time.

Five separate tests make up the GED tests: Language Arts, Writing; Language Arts, Reading; Social Studies; Science; and Mathematics.

Most questions on the tests are multiple choice, but the writing test includes an essay. Some states allow you to take all five sections in one day. Others allow you to break up the test into two parts. It can take a total of seven hours.

1. What is the best summary of the second paragraph of the passage?

A There are many GED testing centers in the United States and Canada. Different centers have different fees. You need to meet age and residency requirements to take the test.

B There are 3,400 GED testing centers in the United States and Canada. A residency requirement means you must live in a certain place.

C The letters *GED* stand for *General Educational Development*.

D There are many testing centers all over the world. You must take the test where you live.

2. What is the best paraphrase of the third paragraph?

F There are two language arts sections but only one each of the other sections.

G There are five separate GED tests for you to choose from.

H The five GED tests are writing, reading, math, science, and social studies.

J There are five GED tests: writing, reading, music, history, and spelling.

Write for Work

Imagine you work for a company that provides information on the GED tests and other tests. You are asked to give information to people who have not read or who have not understood your information. In a notebook, summarize the first paragraph of the article on page 42. Then paraphrase the fourth paragraph in your own words.

 Reading Extension

Turn to "Near Death on the Football Field" on page 26 of *Reading Basics Intermediate 1 Reader*. After you have read and/or listened to the article, answer the questions below.

Circle the letter of the answer to each question.

1. Which sentence would you include in a summary of the article?
   A   Brown wore a brace while he recovered.
   B   It was an important playoff game.
   C   Brown's lips were turning blue.
   D   The team trainer and doctor acted immediately to keep Brown alive.

2. Reread paragraph 9. Which sentence would you include in a paraphrase of the last two sentences of the paragraph?
   F   Lock carefully removed Brown's helmet.
   G   Falb and Lock had to move quickly.
   H   Brown died in Lock's arms.
   J   Falb gently lifted Brown's helmet off.

Write the answer to each item below.

3. Reread paragraph 12. Write a summary of the paragraph.

   _____

   _____

   _____

   _____

4. Reread paragraph 16. Paraphrase the first two sentences.

   _____

   _____

   _____

   _____

Explore Words

HARD AND SOFT g

The letter *g* has two sounds. In the words *shrug* and *gallop*, the letter *g* has a hard sound. In the words *cage* and *giraffe*, the letter *g* has a soft sound. A soft *g* has the same sound as the letter *j*. The letter *g* usually has the soft sound when it is followed by *e*, *i*, or *y*.

Say each word. Then write *hard* or *soft* to show the sound of *g*.

1. gland _____   **4.** magnet _____

2. stage _____   **5.** cigar _____

3. gym _____   **6.** gentle _____

SYLLABLES

Each syllable has one vowel sound. In closed syllables, the vowel usually stands for its short sound (*in*, *thin*). In silent *e* and open syllables, the vowel usually stands for its long sound (*go*, *rate*).

Match each numbered syllable on the left with a lettered syllable on the right to form a word. Write the letter on the line.

_____ **1.** lo   **a.** it   _____ **4.** pro   **a.** ic

_____ **2.** lim   **b.** cate   _____ **5.** ro   **b.** gram

_____ **3.** kit   **c.** ten   _____ **6.** pan   **c.** bot

SPELLING: CONTRACTIONS

A contraction is a short way to write two words. *Aren't* is a contraction. It is a shorter way to write *are not*. Every contraction includes an apostrophe ('). It takes the place of the missing letters. In *I'll*, the apostrophe takes the place of the letters *wi* in *will*.

Write the contraction for each pair of words on the line. Choose from the list in the box.

I'm	we'll	it's	they're	you're	you'll

1. you are _____   **4.** they are _____

2. you will _____   **5.** it is _____

3. we will _____   **6.** I am _____

Antonyms are words that have opposite, or almost opposite, meanings. For example, the words *hot* and *cold* are antonyms.

Match each word on the left with an antonym on the right. Write the letter of the antonym on the line.

_____	**1.**	cruel	**a.**	funny
_____	**2.**	best	**b.**	reject
_____	**3.**	noisy	**c.**	kind
_____	**4.**	tight	**d.**	depart
_____	**5.**	serious	**e.**	worst
_____	**6.**	dangerous	**f.**	safe
_____	**7.**	alive	**g.**	loose
_____	**8.**	accept	**h.**	quiet
_____	**9.**	destroy	**i.**	dead
_____	**10.**	arrive	**j.**	build

ACADEMIC VOCABULARY

Knowing these high-frequency words will help you in many school subjects.

summary   a brief statement of the main points of something

paraphrase   to restate in your own words

reinforce   to strengthen or support

result   a consequence, effect, or outcome of something

exclude   to leave out on purpose

Complete the sentences below using one of the words above.

1. Celia thought carefully about her invitation list; she didn't want to _____ anyone.

2. The back of the book had a good _____ of the story.

3. Repetition helps _____ learning.

4. Claudio couldn't remember the exact quote, but he was able to _____ what was said.

5. The _____ of the boxing match was a draw.

Lesson 1.5

Compare and Contrast

When writers describe two items, they often compare and contrast them. Comparing shows how things are alike, while contrasting shows how things are different. Writers will often compare and contrast within the same passage. They sometimes give clues to let readers know whether they are comparing or contrasting. Below are some clue words and phrases.

Words and Phrases That Show Comparison

| and | both | like | similarly | as | likewise | in the same way |

Words and Phrases That Show Contrast

| but | in contrast | on the other hand | although | however | unlike |

When you read, you may want to organize your thoughts about how two things are similar and how they are different. Making a list or filling in a table like the one below can help you keep track of what you are reading without getting confused.

	How They Are Alike	**How They Are Different**
apples and oranges	fruits, grow on trees, roughly the same size and shape	Apples have cores; oranges do not. Oranges are orange; apples are red, yellow, or green.

Read the passage. Circle the clue words and phrases that show you whether the writer is comparing or contrasting.

> Earth and Venus are about the same size. Earth has a good deal of life and water, but Venus is too hot for life to develop. Venus is the planet closest to Earth and has thick clouds. Similarly, Earth also has clouds. Earth's atmosphere contains oxygen. In contrast, Venus's atmosphere is mostly carbon dioxide. The two planets have about the same mass and density.

How many clue words and phrases did you circle? There are six. *And, similarly, also,* and *about the same* show comparisons. *But* and *in contrast* are used to show contrasts. These words and phrases can help you understand the similarities and differences between the two planets.

Write *compare* if the sentence shows how two things are alike. Write *contrast* if it shows how they are different. Then circle the clue words or phrases that signal comparison or contrast.

_____ **1.** The day was sunny but cooler than expected.

_____ **2.** Fish use gills to take oxygen from water; whales, however, must breathe air.

_____ **3.** Like her sister, Hua had quite a temper.

_____ **4.** Both President Lincoln and President Kennedy were assassinated.

_____ **5.** Fahran can play the piano, although he can't read music.

_____ **6.** I'd like to go out tonight; on the other hand, there's a program on TV I want to watch.

_____ **7.** A butterfly has slender antennae; in contrast, a moth's antennae are thick.

_____ **8.** Unlike air travel, traveling by train offers scenic views of the countryside.

_____ **9.** Wolves in a pack have a pecking order, with one wolf accepted as the leader; similarly, your dog should accept you as "boss."

_____ **10.** Razeen refused to budge in the same way that a stubborn mule digs in its hooves and pulls back.

_____ **11.** The dog could run as fast as a speeding train.

_____ **12.** Esmerelda wanted carrot cake, but Kelley wanted chocolate.

_____ **13.** Unlike most cats who hate the water, many dogs love to swim.

_____ **14.** Like humans, giraffes have only seven bones in their necks.

_____ **15.** Kasem and Daw were both excellent pitchers.

_____ **16.** Tisa was a much better cook than her sister.

_____ **17.** Limes and lemons are both citrus fruits.

_____ **18.** The subway runs every 15 minutes, but the bus only runs every half hour.

_____ **19.** Green Street is a one-way street, and Mason Avenue is as well.

_____ **20.** Aneel ordered a turkey sandwich on rye bread for lunch, and Frankie did likewise.

For each set of information, write two sentences: one that shows how the things are alike and one that shows how the things are different. Use clue words or phrases in your sentences.

1. *the Rocky Mountains:* in North America; tall, sharp peaks; ice capped; younger mountains; rise far above surrounding land

   the Appalachian Mountains: in North America; gently rounded peaks, shorter, worn down by time and erosion; very ancient; rise far above surrounding land

   Alike: _____

   Different: _____

2. *a housefly:* insect, six legs, all have wings, lives independently

   an ant: insect, six legs, most do not have wings, lives in organized communities

   Alike: _____

   Different: _____

3. *a dance class:* all participants move through same steps together, move to music, learn steps to dance for pleasure or for a performance

   an aerobics class: all participants move through same steps together, move to music, keep moving to get fit

   Alike: _____

   Different: _____

4. *a fork:* eating tool; four or five narrow, sharp tines at end to spear food; flat handle fits hand

   a spoon: eating tool; small, shallow bowl at end to lift, stir, or measure food; flat handle fits hand

   Alike: _____

   Different: _____

5. *a pencil:* writing tool; writes with graphite; usually can be erased

   a pen: writing tool; writes with ink; usually permanent and cannot be erased

   Alike: _____

   Different: _____

Read the passage. Then circle the letter of the answer to each question.

(1) Have you heard of the dodo and the blue pigeon? (2) These two birds no longer exist. (3) Both once lived on the island of Mauritius and nowhere else. (4) In many ways, however, the birds were quite different. (5) The dodo was clumsy, and it could not fly. (6) The blue pigeon flew gracefully. (7) The dodo nested on the ground, while the blue pigeon nested in trees. (8) You might think the blue pigeon's differences would have been more useful than the dodo's in protecting it. (9) However, people thought blue pigeons were delicious, so hunters shot them for food and sport. (10) Sadly, blue pigeons became extinct, just as the dodo did.

1. What is the purpose of this passage?

   A to describe why the dodo and the blue pigeon are extinct

   B to compare and contrast the dodo and the blue pigeon

   C to show only how the dodo and the blue pigeon are alike

   D to show only how the dodo and the blue pigeon are different

2. What is one way the two birds were alike?

   F They had the ability to fly.

   G Their nesting habits were the same.

   H They were both very clumsy.

   J They lived only on the island of Mauritius.

3. What is one way the two birds were different?

   A One type was killed off by humans, while the other type still exists.

   B One type is extinct, while the other type is only endangered.

   C Their nesting habits were different.

   D They lived in different locations.

4. Which sentences in the passage show contrasts?

   F sentences 4–7

   G sentences 2, 3, and 9

   H sentences 2 and 10

   J sentences 1, 4, and 8

5. Which sentences in the passage compare similarities?

   A sentences 4–7

   B sentences 2, 3, and 10

   C sentences 5 and 10

   D sentences 1, 4, and 8

Workplace Skill:
Compare and Contrast Information in a Graph

One way companies look at and keep track of information is by using graphs. A bar graph has bars that show an amount or a value. Bar graphs compare two or more things. To understand a graph, start by reading the title. It will usually be above the graph. It will show you what the subject of the graph is.

Read the graph. Then circle the letter of the answer to each question.

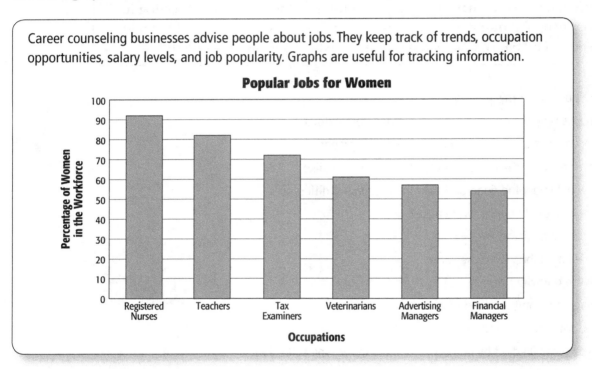

Career counseling businesses advise people about jobs. They keep track of trends, occupation opportunities, salary levels, and job popularity. Graphs are useful for tracking information.

1. What does each bar of the graph show you?

 A the percentage of women within a particular occupation

 B the percentage of salary levels for each occupation

 C the number of women employed in each occupation

 D the reason each particular occupation is popular

2. Which job has the third highest percentage of women performing it?

 F registered nurse

 G financial manager

 H tax examiner

 J veterinarian

3. What job on the graph has the lowest percentage of women performing it?

 A tax examiner

 B veteranarian

 C financial manager

 D teacher

4. Which occupation has a higher percentage of women performing it than teacher?

 F advertising manager

 G registered nurse

 H tax examiner

 J veterinarian

Write for Work

Graphs present information in a visual form. Study the graph on page 50. In a notebook, write a paragraph about what information is presented in the graph. Include information on how the graph can be important for future job seekers.

 Reading Extension

Turn to "The Mysterious Life of Twins" on page 34 of *Reading Basics Intermediate 1 Reader*. After you have read and/or listened to the article, answer the questions below.

Circle the letter of the answer to each question.

1. What is one thing Daphne Goodship and Barbara Hebert had in common?
   A   Both wore rubber bands around their wrists.
   B   They said they could feel each other's pain.
   C   They both divorced and remarried.
   D   They both met their husbands at local dances.

2. Which twins thought they could sense when the other was in trouble?
   F   Jim and Jim
   G   Brenda and Daphne
   H   Ron and Rod
   J   Andreina and Andreini

3. What is the one difference given between the "Jim" twins?
   A   One Jim married a woman named Betty, and the other Jim married a woman named Betsy.
   B   One Jim named his son James Alan, and the other Jim named his son James Allan.
   C   One Jim had a pet dog named Joy, and the other Jim had a pet dog named Toy.
   D   One Jim liked to vacation on the beach, and the other Jim liked to vacation at amusement parks.

Write the answer to each question.

4. What is one way that all of the sets of twins in this article were similar?

   _____

   _____

5. What is one way that Jack Yufe and Oskar Stöhr were similar?

   _____

   _____

Explore Words

The letter *x* can stand for the sounds of *ks* as in *box*. It can also stand for the sounds of *gz* as in *exit*. The *gz* sounds usually happen when *x* falls between two vowels.

Say each word. Then write either *ks* or *gz* on the line to show which sounds *x* stands for in that word.

1. fox _____
2. exam _____
3. exhibit _____
4. tax _____

5. exist _____
6. exact _____
7. relax _____
8. climax _____

COMPOUND WORDS

Compound words are words made up of two separate words. For example, *doghouse* is made up of the word *dog* and the word *house*.

Combine the words to make a compound word. Write the compound word on the line.

1. book + mark = _____
2. book + case = _____
3. check + list = _____
4. check + book = _____

SPELLING: PLURALS

Some words can be made plural by adding *-s* to them: for example, *diner/diners*. Add *-es* to words that end in *s, ss, sh, x,* or *ch*: for example, *address/addresses*.

Write *-s* or *-es* to form the plural of each word.

1. coupon _____
2. student _____
3. dish _____
4. teacher _____

5. church _____
6. dress _____
7. tax _____
8. bus _____

The letters *-er* and *-est* can be added to the end of words. The ending *-er* means "more" and is used to compare two things. The ending *-est* means "most" and is used to compare three or more things.

A horse's neck is *longer* than a hippo's. A giraffe has the *longest* neck of all.

For each word, form two new words by adding *-er* and *-est*. Then use one of the new words in a sentence.

1. long _____ _____

_____

2. loud _____ _____

_____

3. small _____ _____

_____

4. thick _____ _____

_____

ACADEMIC VOCABULARY

Knowing these high-frequency words will help you in many school subjects.

compare to show how things are alike

contrast to show how things are different

clue a fact or idea that serves as a guide

organize to arrange

similar alike without being identical

Complete the sentences below using one of the words above.

1. It was easy to _____ the two girls; they were nothing alike.

2. Adara's favorite sweater ripped, so she tried to find one that was _____.

3. The inspector found a _____ that helped him solve the mystery.

4. Juan decided to _____ the features of both cars he wanted.

5. Nala wanted to _____ her books by topic and author.

Lesson 1.6

Use Forms

You fill out forms to provide information. There are many different types of forms. For example, a job application is a form. A customer survey is a form. When you shop online, you fill out a form to give your address and payment information. Some forms have blank lines for you to fill in. Others have a list with boxes for you to check.

Different sections of forms ask for different types of information. For example, you may put your name and address at the top of a form and your medical history at the bottom. Some forms have sections that say *For official use only* or *Do not write here*. That means that part of the form needs to be filled in by the person who receives it. You should skip those sections. Many forms abbreviate words or use short phrases when asking for information. It is important to understand these phrases or abbreviations.

Make sure to read the whole form before you start to write. Look up any words you don't know, or have someone clarify meanings for things you don't understand.

The form below is part of an application for a credit card. Read the form and decide if you should write in cursive. Then decide if there is any part of the form you should not fill in. Do not complete the form.

(Please Print)

Name (last name, first name)   SS#

Street Address   City   State   ZIP Code

Years There   Own/Rent

Annual Income $ _____

For official use only

Credit Score_____

Card Number _____   Expiration Date _____

You should not write in cursive. Did you see the instructions at the top? They say *Please Print*. Printing ensures that the person who receives your form can read it. The bottom of the form says *For official use only*. This tells you not to fill in this section.

Reread the credit card application form on page 54. Then answer the questions below.

1. What does the abbreviation SS# stand for? _____

2. If you make about $2,000 a month, what amount should you write for your annual income? _____

3. If your name were Anna Diaz, how would you write your name on this form? _____

Read the customer survey. Then answer the questions. Do not answer the survey questions.

Tell us about your visit to Woodman's Restaurant

1. Date of visit _____

2. How many people were in your party? _____

3. How do you rate the following? *(circle your answer)*

Speed of service	**Very Good**	**Good**	**OK**	**Poor**	**Very Poor**
Cleanliness	**Very Good**	**Good**	**OK**	**Poor**	**Very Poor**
Quality of food	**Very Good**	**Good**	**OK**	**Poor**	**Very Poor**
Choice of food	**Very Good**	**Good**	**OK**	**Poor**	**Very Poor**

4. How do you rate the overall performance of this restaurant? _____
(use a score of 10 for excellent and 1 for poor)

5. Are there any other comments that you would like to make?

_____

_____

---

4. If your food took a long time to arrive, what might you circle after *speed of service*?

A Very Good

B Good

C OK

D Poor

5. If you felt the overall performance of the restaurant was excellent, what should you write for question 4?

F Excellent

G 10

H 1

J Very Good

The form below is part of an application for health insurance. Read the form but do not fill it out. Then answer the questions below.

---

22. Ht. _____ Wt. _____   Ht. _____ Wt. _____
    Proposed Insured   Spouse

---

23. Has Weight Changed More Than 10 Pounds in Last Year?
    Proposed Insured   Yes   No   Spouse   Yes   No

---

24. Ever Smoked?
    Proposed Insured   Yes   No   Spouse   Yes   No

    How Many Per Day?
    Proposed Insured _____ Spouse _____

---

25. Last Doctor Consultation:
    Proposed Insured _____ Spouse _____
    Reason:
    Proposed Insured

    _____

    Spouse

    _____

---

1. Who is *proposed insured*?

_____

2. What should an applicant write in the *spouse* area if he or she is unmarried?

_____

3. What do *ht.* and *wt.* stand for?

_____

4. What should the applicant do with the words *Yes* and *No* on the form?

_____

5. What should the applicant write under *Last Doctor Consultation*?

_____

Read the form below but do not fill it out. Then circle the letter of the answer to each question.

BILL TO:
Name _____
Address _____
_____
City _____
State _____ ZIP _____ Country _____
Phone Number _____
E-mail _____

SHIP TO: (Only if different from "Bill To.")
First Name/Initial   Last Name
_____   _____
Address _____
_____
City _____
State _____ ZIP _____ Country _____

Item Number   Page   Description   Size   Color   Qty.   Price
_____   _____   _____   _____   _____   _____   _____
_____   _____   _____   _____   _____   _____   _____

Total prices _____

Sales tax _____

Method of Payment
Check or money order enclosed _____   TOTAL _____
Charge to my (*check one*):
Visa _____ MasterCard _____ American Express _____
Credit Card Number _____ Expiration Date: Month _____ Year _____
_____
Signature (as shown on credit card)

---

1. When might you need to fill out a form like this?

 A if you are placing a catalog order by phone

 B if you are placing a catalog order by mail

 C if you are sending a package out of town

 D if you are placing an order online

2. What should you put under "Qty."?

 F the number of quarts of something you are ordering

 G the number of items described in the row that you want to buy

 H a ✓ to indicate that you want the best quality available

 J an asterisk if you are going to write a special note below

3. When would you need to fill out the "Ship to" section?

 A if you want the company to send your order instead of you picking it up

 B if you want the order shipped to another country

 C if your shipping address is the same as your billing address

 D if your shipping address is different from your billing address

Workplace Skill: Use a Job Application Form

Many businesses use forms to help them keep track of information. Before you fill out a form, read it over. If you don't have your facts available, it can take more time to fill one out. You will have to find the information.

Read the job application form but do not fill it out. Then circle the letter of the answer to each question.

Personal Data	Date

Applying for position as _____
Salary required _____ Date available _____
Name _____
Address _____
E-mail address _____ Telephone _____
Social Security No. _____
Are you legally entitled to work in the United States?   Yes ❑   No ❑

Education

High school _____
Specialized training _____
Other education _____

Skills

List any special skills you may have, including any obtained in the military.
_____
_____

1. What piece of information does this application form ask you to provide?

   A   a date of birth

   B   a reference

   C   a salary requirement

   D   a former employer

2. The word *legally* as used in the form means

   F   in accordance with laws.

   G   without permission.

   H   with the consent of the employer.

   J   required by the Human Resources department.

3. If you know shorthand, where would you write that?

   A   next to "High school"

   B   under "Skills"

   C   in the margin

   D   You should not write it on the form.

4. What should you do if you do not have an e-mail address?

   F   leave that line blank

   G   make an e-mail address up

   H   rewrite your phone number

   J   rewrite your mailing address

Write for Work

Imagine you are applying for a job. Use the sample job application form on page 58 to practice filling in a job application. Write your responses in a notebook. Provide as many details as you can. As you fill out the application, be aware of the kinds of information you are asked to supply.

Workplace Extension

The New Job

Jamal Williams tried not to panic, but that was easier said than done. It was his first day on the job at the Big Bag Grocery Store, and the man who was supposed to train him called in sick.

Now his new boss, Mr. Gregor, wanted him to stock the dairy shelves with a shipment of milk that had just arrived. There were several types of milk. They all came in different sizes: gallons, half gallons, quarts, and pints.

"This shouldn't take you too long, Jamal," Mr. Gregor said. "Put the milk that's already on the shelves in the front. Put the new milk in the back. Read the expiration dates. If you see any stale milk, yank it from the shelves altogether. I've got a ton of work to do, so I'll be in my office in the back. You're on your own."

Circle the letter of the answer to each question.

1. What is an expiration date?

   A the date the article was first manufactured

   B the date the article was delivered to the store

   C the date when the article was placed on the shelf

   D the date after which something should not be sold

2. What is Jamal's main problem?

   F He does not want to work at the grocery store.

   G He has no one to train him on his first day.

   H He does not like Mr. Gregor.

   J He has not met his new boss yet.

Write the answer to the question.

3. What should Jamal do if a customer interrupts his work to ask a question?

_____

_____

_____

Explore Words

CONSONANT PAIRS *wr, kn, gn*

Some consonant pairs include a silent letter. In the combinations *wr*, *kn*, and *gn*, the first letter in each pair is silent. Together, these consonant pairs stand for only one sound—the sound of the second letter.

Use *wr*, *kn*, or *gn* to complete each word. The first item has been done for you.

1. Ana swatted at a ___*gn*___ at flying near her.

2. The doorbell was broken, so Isolda _____ocked.

3. The skater fell and sprained his _____ist.

4. It is really hard to desi_____ a dress.

5. Julia _____ote a note to her aunt.

6. Gina _____ew the answer right away.

LONG *e* SPELLED -*y*

The letter *y* can sometimes stands for the long *e* vowel sound, as in the word *very*.

Circle the word with the long *e* sound that completes each sentence.

1. Luis would (study, cry) before a test.

2. The torn old photo looked (ugly, dry).

3. Do you have (my, any) stamps?

4. Jimiyu has a very nice (butterfly, family).

CONTEXT CLUES

You can use context clues to understand the meaning of an unfamiliar word. Context clues are hints in the same sentence or in the surrounding sentences or paragraphs.

Read the sentences below. Use context clues to figure out the meaning of each underlined word. Then write the meaning on the line.

1. Alejandro stayed up late. The next day, he felt <u>sluggish</u>, or tired.

   _____

2. Ships sail over the <u>high seas</u>—the open waters that do not belong to any nation.

   _____

3. In some places in the ocean, sailboats are often <u>stalled</u> because there is no wind to move them.

   _____

4. Lujayn's flaky ride left her <u>stranded</u> at the mall with no way to get home.

   _____

Possessive words show who or what owns something. To make a singular noun possessive, add 's to the end of the word. *The boy's voice is changing*. The 's shows you the changing voice belongs to one boy. Add s' to the end of a plural noun to show possession. *The boys' hats were stolen*. The s' shows you the stolen hats belong to more than one boy.

Show ownership in the following sentences by adding 's or s' to the underlined words. Write the possessive word on the line. The first item has been done for you.

1. Carly _____ *Carly's* _____ book is about animals.

2. Many <u>dog</u> _____ bones were buried there.

3. A mouse was in the <u>hawk</u> _____ beak.

4. Mi Hi heard two wild <u>turkey</u> _____ voices at once.

5. The red <u>fox</u> _____ paw was stuck under the roots.

6. His <u>father</u> _____ name is Chetan.

7. All of the <u>girl</u> _____ schedules were very similar.

8. The <u>twin</u> _____ teachers couldn't tell the boys apart.

ACADEMIC VOCABULARY

Knowing these high-frequency words will help you in many school subjects.

form	a document with blank spaces for information to be entered
survey	a set of questions used to gather information or opinions
medical	relating to medicine
abbreviate	to shorten
clarify	to make more easily understood

Complete the sentences below using one of the words above.

1. The _____ got information about people's opinions of the candidate.

2. The post office asks people to _____ state names in a certain way.

3. The doctor worked for years to get his _____ degree.

4. Binta needed to fill out the right _____ to file her taxes.

5. Soledad couldn't understand the instructions, so she asked the teacher to _____ them.

Lesson 1.7

Find the Main Idea

The main idea of a paragraph is the most important idea. It is the point the writer is trying to make about the subject. Facts, examples, and other details in a paragraph usually support the main idea.

The main idea may be stated in a topic sentence. The topic sentence may be the first sentence, or it may be a sentence in another part of the paragraph. The main idea may also not be stated at all. When the main idea isn't stated, readers must identify the main idea by using information that is given in the text.

When you have identified the main idea, read the rest of the passage. Examine the relationship between the main idea and details. If the details do not support the main idea, try stating the main idea in a different way. Read the example:

> Whales live in the ocean, but they are not fish. Whales are mammals that come to the surface to breathe. When they are underwater, they must hold their breath like other mammals do. When the whale finally surfaces, it blows this air out through the blowhole in the top of its head. Then it draws in fresh air through its blowhole.

The main idea of the passage above might be stated, "Because whales are mammals, they need to breathe oxygen like all mammals do." The details support the main idea by explaining how whales breathe in and out.

Read the passage. Underline the main idea.

> Today the lion is often called the king of the beasts. The original king of the beasts, however, was *Tyrannosaurus rex,* a huge meat-eating dinosaur. The name *Tyrannosaurus rex* means "king of the tyrant lizards." *Tyrannosaurus rex* was twice as large as an elephant. Its head was more than four feet long. It had sharp teeth and claws. It was a meat-eater and hunted for prey. Experts say it could run fast despite its size. Like all dinosaurs, *Tyrannosaurus rex* is now extinct.

Did you underline the second sentence? The main idea of the passage is that the *Tyrannosaurus rex* was the king of dinosaurs, or the biggest and most ferocious. The details that describe the dinosaur's size and other physical traits support this idea.

Notice that not all the details in the passage support the main idea. The last sentence, *Like all dinosaurs,* Tyrannosaurus rex *is now extinct,* is an interesting fact, but it is not necessary to understanding the main idea of the passage.

Read each passage. Then circle the letter of the sentence that restates the main idea.

Many people fly their country's flag on holidays. Other people do this year round. Most people fly their flags as a way to show respect for their countries, yet many people do not know how to properly care for the flags. For example, when flags become dull and dirty, they should be washed. However, some people never wash them. They think it is disrespectful to get flags wet. This isn't true. Most official flags are washed regularly. Keeping a flag clean shows respect for the flag and the country.

1. **A**   Dirty flags should be washed.

   B   Some people think it is not respectful to wash flags.

   C   There are ways to take care of flags to show respect for them.

   D   Many people do not fly flags year round.

Alfred Hitchcock has been called the master of suspense films. He directed many classic movies. These include *Psycho, The Birds,* and *Dial M for Murder.* His movies kept audiences on the edge of their seats. Hitchcock planned his films very carefully. He thought out every shot in detail long before the cameras rolled. It was said that Hitchcock did most of his moviemaking in his head, not through a camera.

2. **F**   Alfred Hitchcock was a master at making suspense films.

   G   Alfred Hitchcock directed many classic movies.

   H   Alfred Hitchcock planned his movies shortly before they were filmed.

   J   Alfred Hitchcock's movies kept viewers on the edge of their seats.

Crocodiles will eat most kinds of birds, but according to folk tales, there is one kind they won't eat. It's a bird called the zic-zac, and it gets and gives special treatment. When a crocodile comes ashore, it opens its mouth. The zic-zac climbs inside without fear and eats the leeches that have attached themselves to the inside of the crocodile's mouth. The zic-zac gets a good meal. The crocodile gets a clean mouth.

3. **A**   Animals have various ways of helping each other.

   B   The zic-zac and the crocodile help one another.

   C   Zic-zacs enjoy eating leeches.

   D   Crocodiles will put up with a lot for clean teeth.

Read each passage. Write the main idea. Then write one detail that supports the main idea.

In 2009 some people in Michigan made a large slab of fudge. At the time, it was the largest slab of fudge ever made. It measured 8 feet by 36.3 feet and weighed 5,200 pounds. This fudge used lots of ingredients and took 50 people more than two days to make. It was later sold in one-pound pieces for charity.

1. **Main Idea**

   _____

2. **Detail**

   _____

When your foot "falls asleep," it's not because it is tired. A foot falls asleep when it doesn't get enough blood. Blood flows to the foot through blood vessels in the leg. When you sit on your foot, you block off the blood vessels. Nerve endings can also get blocked. The "pins and needles" you feel as your foot wakes up are the nerves going back to work.

3. **Main Idea**

   _____

4. **Detail**

   _____

California condors are disappearing because of humans. People have taken much of the forest land where condors live. Poisons used by farmers have also killed some of these giant birds. Not many baby condors are born each year. Laws protect them, but people fear the condors will soon become extinct.

5. **Main Idea**

   _____

6. **Detail**

   _____

Read the passage. Then circle the letter of the answer to each question.

(1) Most frozen food has been treated to kill the germs that would cause it to spoil. (2) Food that has been thawed and exposed to air is likely to spoil. (3) Freezing food that has been exposed to air will not kill those germs. (4) It will only slow their growth. (5) Food experts say that you should never refreeze food that has thawed outside of the refrigerator. (6) You should cook and eat thawed food soon after thawing. (7) That way, it won't spoil and cause food poisoning.

1. What is the passage about?

   A the danger of food poisoning

   B selecting a good freezer

   C the danger of refreezing thawed food

   D how germs cause food to spoil

2. Which of the following details would fit this passage?

   F how many people purchase frozen foods

   G why fresh food is better than frozen food

   H how to keep germs out of thawed food

   J why you should cook pork well

3. Which sentence best states the main idea of the passage?

   A Frozen food that has thawed should not be refrozen.

   B Most frozen food has been treated to kill germs.

   C Eat only fresh foods because frozen foods contain germs.

   D Germs are everywhere, and they cause food to spoil.

4. The main idea of the passage is best summed up in which sentence in the passage?

   F sentence 1

   G sentence 3

   H sentence 5

   J sentence 6

5. What makes your answer choice for item 4 the best main idea sentence?

   A It contains a new idea.

   B It supports the main idea.

   C It states the most important idea of the passage.

   D It has no errors.

Workplace Skill: Find the Main Idea in an Article

The main idea of a passage is the most important idea. Other sentences in the passage give details and examples about the main idea.

Read the article. Then circle the letter of the answer to each question.

What Is Good about a Government Job?

There are good reasons to think about a public-sector job. For one thing, your employer will not go out of business! We will always need our government. Of course, you may lose your job for other reasons, but you could try to get another government job.

Most government jobs have good benefits. If you work full-time, you will probably have health insurance. You will also have paid sick days and vacation time. If you stay in your job for a long time, you will probably also have money for your retirement.

Laws and rules protect you. All job openings must be advertised. Job duties and pay must be stated publicly, too. Sometimes it is good to have clear rules about the job and the rate of pay. The boss has to follow the rules. Everyone gets the same treatment.

Finally, like other large employers, the city or the county may help with your education. You might get to study during work time. You might get free on-the-job skills training, or you might get money to help cover college costs.

So if you are job hunting, don't forget the public sector. If you work for your government, it may work for you!

1. What is the main idea of the article?
   A A government job is better than working for a business.
   B Government jobs provide the best benefits.
   C It is easy to find a government job.
   D A government job might be right for you.

2. As used in the article, the word *retirement* means
   F "when you are older and no longer working."
   G "when you go to bed early."
   H "when you go away to rest or be alone."
   J "when you prepare a financial budget."

Write for Work

You are thinking about applying for a government job that a friend told you about. In a notebook, list the things you think are benefits of working for the government. List the things you think you might not like about working for the government.

Workplace Extension

Responding to a Boss

Lewis Payne had started a new job. The pay wasn't great, but the job was full-time with benefits. He felt lucky to get a job at all after he quit high school early. Lewis liked his boss, and the boss seemed to like Lewis, too. After six months, Lewis went to the office to pick up his paycheck. His boss said, "You're a hard worker and a smart young man. You could have a good future if you had an education. Why don't you go back to school? You can even study on work time. Let me know if you want to try it." Lewis knew the boss was right that he wouldn't get a better job unless he improved his reading and writing.

Circle the letter of the answer to each question.

1. What would be the best way for Lewis to respond to his boss's suggestion?

   A to tell her she should not be so critical of his skills

   B to tell her he does not like school and does not plan to go back

   C to tell her he would think seriously about her suggestion

   D to tell other employees that he thinks she should mind her own business

2. Lewis's boss is trying to be

   F unfriendly.

   G critical.

   H dismissive.

   J supportive.

Write the answer to each question.

3. Why does Lewis feel lucky that he got a job?

_____

4. If Lewis wants to get a better job in the future, what do you think he needs to do?

_____

Explore Words

CONSONANT PAIR *sc*

The consonant pair *sc* can make different sounds. When *sc* is followed by *a, o,* or *u,* as in *scoop,* the letters stand for two sounds: *s* and a hard *c.* When *sc* is followed by *e, i,* or *y,* as in *scent,* the letters combine to stand for one sound: *s.*

Read each word. Then write *one sound* or *two sounds* on the line.

1. scale _____

2. ascend _____

3. scab _____

4. scuff _____

5. scythe _____

6. scorn _____

LONG *i* SPELLED *-y*

Sometimes the letter *y* stands for the long *i* sound, as in *spry* or *fry.*

Circle the word with the long *i* sound that completes each sentence.

1. Let's (pry, empty) the nail out of the board.

2. Look to the (library, sky) to see the stars.

3. Sheila wants to (apply, study) for the job.

4. Afra was too (shy, pretty) to speak up.

5. Do not be afraid to (try, hurry) new things.

6. She was sad, but she didn't want to (pity, cry).

CONTEXT CLUES

You can sometimes use context clues to understand the meaning of unfamiliar words.

Read the passage. Then answer the questions about the underlined words.

Parrots are known as the birds that can talk. In fact, pet parrots can <u>mimic</u> the speech of humans. They can be taught to say anything their owners <u>fancy</u>. However, they can't learn to <u>express</u> their own ideas. They are merely <u>imitators</u>.

1. What does *mimic* mean?

   a. copy

   b. learn

2. What does *fancy* mean?

   a. expensive

   b. want

3. What does *express* mean?

   a think about

   b. put into words

4. What does *imitator* mean?

   a. something that copies something else

   b. a wild bird

MULTIPLE-MEANING WORDS

Some words have multiple meanings, or more than one meaning. When you read, you need to know which meaning of a word is used in a specific sentence. You can often use context clues in the sentence to figure that out. The word *present* has multiple meanings. Read this sentence: *Antoine grew up in Texas, but at the present time, he is living in New York.* Context clues help you determine that *present* means "occurring now."

Read each sentence. Then circle the letter that gives the meaning of the underlined word.

1. Cintia stood in <u>line</u> to buy movie tickets.
   a. a mark drawn on paper
   b. an arrangement of people in a series

2. Cruz had to pay a parking <u>fine</u>.
   a. a bill charged for breaking the law
   b. good

3. The scarf was bright <u>orange</u>.
   a. a fruit to eat
   b. a color

4. The boys threw pennies in the wishing <u>well</u>.
   a. healthy
   b. a place to get water

5. Alexis went to the <u>fair</u> to go on rides.
   a. following the rules
   b. carnival

6. Taeko had a sprained arm after her <u>fall</u>.
   a. a sudden uncontrollable descent
   b. autumn

7. The waves caused the ship to <u>rock</u>.
   a. to move gently from side to side
   b. a stone

8. There are swings at the <u>park</u>.
   a. to leave a car or vehicle
   b. a large public green area

ACADEMIC VOCABULARY

Knowing these high-frequency words will help you in many school subjects.

point	an idea put forth by someone in a discussion
example	a thing usual of its kind or showing a general rule
identify	to establish or point out who or what
examine	to look over in detail
relationship	the way in which two or more things or people are connected

Complete the sentences below using one of the words above.

1. Mongo tried to use a lot of statistics and facts to prove his _____.

2. The witness had to _____ the suspect in a lineup.

3. The jeweler had to _____ the diamond with a special machine to see if it was fake.

4. Kanika had to give more than one _____ before anyone would believe her argument.

5. He could not find a _____ between height and basketball ability.

Unit 1 Review

Recognize and Recall Details

Every passage has a topic. Details support the topic and give more information about it. Some details may be facts, and other details may be descriptions. Recalling details can help you understand and remember what you have read.

Understand Stated Concepts

Often facts and ideas are stated directly in a passage. You should note which concepts are stated directly and which concepts you inferred. This will help you better understand important facts and details.

Draw Conclusions

When you draw a conclusion from a passage, you figure out its meaning by using information in the passage and your own experience. Conclusions should be valid—that is, they should be supported by facts in the passage. A conclusion that does not make sense or is not supported is an invalid conclusion.

Summarize and Paraphrase

When you summarize a passage, you state the main idea and most important details. A summary is shorter than the original passage. When you paraphrase, you restate a passage in your own words and include most details. It should be about the same length as the original passage.

Compare and Contrast

Comparison shows how two or more things are alike. Contrast shows how two or more things are different. Writers often compare and contrast in the same passage. Clue words can help you identify comparison and contrast.

Use Forms

Forms require information. They can be on paper or online. You complete forms for many reasons, such as obtaining a credit card, applying for a job, or paying taxes. Many forms use abbreviations to save space. It is important to follow all directions when filling out a form.

Find the Main Idea

The main idea is the most important idea in a paragraph or passage. The details in a paragraph support the main idea. It may be stated in a topic sentence, or it may be implied. If it is stated, it may be located anywhere in the paragraph or passage.

Unit 1 Assessment

Read each passage. Then circle the letter of the answer to each question.

> Blood donors are needed all the time. Blood donors save lives. Over 13 million pints of blood are used each year in the United States, but donated blood cannot be stored for long. Most red blood cells can be refrigerated for up to 42 days. Plasma, another blood part, can be frozen for up to one year.

1. What is the main idea of this passage?

   A Blood does not last long after it is donated.

   B New blood donations are needed all the time.

   C Plasma can be refrigerated longer than red blood cells.

   D Blood donors save lives.

2. What is one difference between red blood cells and plasma?

   F Plasma can be frozen for a year, but red blood cells can last only six weeks.

   G Plasma is not as useful as red blood cells.

   H Red blood cells can be frozen for a year, but plasma lasts just six weeks.

   J It is less difficult to donate plasma than red blood cells.

3. Which of the following is the best paraphrase of the passage?

   A Blood donors save lives. Donated blood lasts only six weeks, but it can be frozen for up to a year.

   B It is very important to give blood because it does not last long.

   C People are always needed for giving blood, which saves lives. Millions of pints of blood are used each year in the United States, but blood does not last long. Red blood cells can be refrigerated for six weeks, but plasma can be frozen for a year.

   D Millions of pints of blood are used each year. They have to be used quickly, because donated blood cannot be stored well. It can be frozen for a long time, but otherwise it turns bad quickly.

> The mayfly can live for up to two years but flies for only one day—its last. The mayfly spends most of its life in the water, as a nymph. During this time, it eats and grows and sheds its skin many times. When the nymph matures, it sheds its skin one last time and develops wings. Then it flies away, mates, and dies—all in one day. This stage of an adult mayfly is so short that the mayfly doesn't need to eat. Therefore, the mouths of adult mayflies do not fully develop.

4. Which of these is the best summary of the passage?

   F The mayfly spends two years eating and growing as a nymph. It lives in the water. Then it grows wings, flies away, and mates. Then it dies without eating.

   G The mayfly spends most of its time as a nymph.

   H The mayfly's adult life is short. It spends most of its time in the water, and the adult mayfly has an undeveloped mouth.

   J The mayfly spends most of its life as a nymph. In one day it begins to fly, mates, and dies.

A fly may look harmless, but it isn't. It is one of the dirtiest creatures on Earth. Flies lay their eggs in garbage, waste, and rotting flesh. They eat spoiled food. Each fly carries thousands of germs that can cause disease. Flies spread these germs to people when they land on food. These germ-carrying insects also reproduce very quickly.

5. What is the main idea of this passage?

   A Every fly carries germs.

   B Flies eat spoiled food, waste, and rotting flesh.

   C Flies reproduce quickly even though they carry germs.

   D There is no way to get rid of flies.

6. From this passage you can conclude that

   F you should not let food spoil.

   G you should be careful not to let flies sit on food.

   H flies are harmless.

   J flies spread germs only when they bite you.

Among honeybees, the worker bees are the busiest. Worker bees clean the hive in the beginning of their adult lives. They build the hive and guard it against danger. They fly from plant to plant in search of food. All worker bees are females. The queen is the head of the hive. Her job is to lay eggs in the spring. The only function of male bees, or drones, is to mate with queens. Drones are present in the hive only during the summer. Food becomes scarce in the fall. Workers drag the drones out of the hive and stop feeding them. Without food and shelter, the drones die.

7. How are the worker bees and queen bees alike?

   A They lay eggs.

   B They gather food.

   C They are female bees.

   D They are in the hive only during the summer.

8. Which detail from the passage supports the idea that worker bees are the busiest bees in the hive?

   F The queen is the head of the hive.

   G The queen lays the eggs.

   H The drones get food from the workers in the summer.

   J Worker bees build and guard the hive.

Read the form but do not fill it out. Then circle the letter of the answer to each question.

Employee Contact Information

First Name _____ Middle Name _____ Last Name _____

Address _____ Home E-mail _____ Home Phone _____

City _____ Date of Birth _____ Cell Phone _____

State _____ Emergency Contact Name _____

ZIP Code _____ Emergency Contact Phone _____
_____

Automobile Information

Make _____ Model _____

License Plate Number _____ State _____
_____

For office use only

Employee Number _____ Include in directory ☐ yes ☐ no

---

9. If you are an employee, what should you write on the line for *Employee Number*?

   A nothing

   B your phone number

   C the number of employees in your section

   D the location of your workstation

10. Why does the form ask for the state in the Automobile Information section?

   F The employer wants to know what state you live in.

   G The employer wants to know what state you bought your car in.

   H Different states can give the same license plate numbers.

   J Driver's licenses have different designs in different states.

11. What is the purpose of the emergency contact?

   A It's the name of someone you should call if someone else at work has an emergency.

   B If you have an emergency, the employer needs to know whom to call.

   C It's the person who is in charge if there is an emergency.

   D The employer wants to keep track of its employees.

12. If you have a cell phone but no home phone, what should you do?

   F Make up a phone number.

   G Promise to have a home phone installed.

   H Write a friend's phone number.

   J Leave the home phone line blank or draw a line through it.

Read the memo. Then circle the letter of the answer to each question.

> **From:** Human Resources
> **To:** All Employees
> **Subject:** Fire Drill Reminder
>
> There will be a fire drill on Friday, May 8. Please make sure that all employees know the fire procedures ahead of time.
>
> - The emergency exits are located on either end of the factory floor: near the lunchroom and near the storage room.
> - When the alarm sounds, immediately exit the factory by going out the nearest exit.
> - All employees should meet near the picnic table on the grass after exiting the building.
> - Our fire marshal is Karen Winke. She will have a list of all employees. Make sure to check in with her.
> - Wait patiently for the fire department to tell us it is safe to return inside.

13. What is the first thing you should do when the alarm sounds?

   A Check in with Karen Winke.

   B Meet at the picnic table.

   C Leave the factory by the nearest exit.

   D Wait for the fire department.

14. Look at the fourth and fifth bullets. What conclusion can you draw about why the company wants everyone to wait together?

   F The picnic table is a convenient place to eat lunch.

   G They want to make sure everyone has left the building safely.

   H They want employees to discuss work while they wait.

   J Karen likes to be in charge of things.

15. Where are the emergency exits?

   A near the restroom and near the lunchroom

   B near the lockers and by the picnic table

   C near Karen Winke's office and near the restroom

   D near the lunchroom and near the storage room

16. How would you summarize this memo for a coworker?

   F When the fire alarm sounds, walk out the exit to the picnic tables and check in with Karen Winke. Then wait for the fire department.

   G It is important to know what to do during the fire drill.

   H Do not panic during a fire alarm. Find the emergency exit closest to you. Wait by the picnic table on the grass. Karen Winke will have a list of all employees. She's the fire marshal. Check in with her and wait for the fire department.

   J There will be a fire drill on May 8. Make sure you know where the emergency exits are and where to meet when you get outside. You will have to check in with the fire marshal.

Read the bulletin board notice. Then circle the letter of the answer to each question.

Overtime

TownGroup is changing its policies on overtime. From now on, all overtime must be approved in advance by a manager. This is to prevent excessive overtime usage. In the past four months, overtime hours have more than doubled.

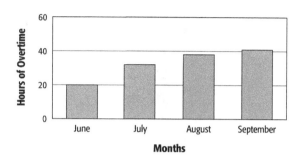

While we know that fall is our busiest season, TownGroup will no longer allow any overtime without prior approval. To receive approval, submit the overtime request form to your supervisor. There are copies in the HR office as well as on the bulletin board in the lunchroom. Include the reason that you need to work overtime as well as the amount of time you estimate it will take you.

This is a change from past practices in which overtime was performed at the employee's discretion. Please place this page in your employee handbook for future reference.

17. What is the main idea of this page?

  A It costs TownGroup a lot of money to pay for excessive overtime.

  B Employees should be able to complete their work during regular hours.

  C Employees abused the overtime policy in the past.

  D All overtime must be approved by a manager.

18. What reason does TownGroup state for changing its policy?

  F TownGroup wants to prevent excessive overtime.

  G Fall is the busiest season.

  H TownGroup cannot afford to pay for all the overtime.

  J It is easy to submit the form.

19. How is the new policy different from the previous overtime policy?

  A The old forms did not ask for an estimated time, while the new forms do.

  B Approval is easier to get under the new policy.

  C Under the old policy, no approval was required to work overtime, while approval is required under the new policy.

  D Under the old policy, forms were kept in the managers' offices, while under the new policy, they are in the HR office and the lunchroom.

20. How many hours of overtime were worked in June?

  F 20

  G 32

  H 38

  J 131

Circle the letter of the answer to each question.

21. Which word is a contraction of *have* and *not*?

    A haven'ot

    B havn't

    C havenot

    D haven't

22. Which word has the soft *c* sound?

    F cast

    G cell

    H coal

    J cub

23. Which word is a synonym for *hot*?

    A cold

    B purple

    C fiery

    D sun

24. Which word is an antonym for *generous*?

    F stingy

    G wealthy

    H kind

    J noble

25. Which phrase means "the pens belonging to several writers"?

    A the writer's pens

    B the writers's pens

    C the writers' pens

    D the writers pens

26. Which word fits into both sentences?

    The safety _____ on the bottle of aspirin was broken.

    We watched the _____ at the aquarium.

    F show

    G penguin

    H seal

    J cap

27. In which word does the *sc* pair stand for two sounds?

    A scent

    B scene

    C science

    D scanty

28. Which word has a silent letter?

    F cram

    G scar

    H sign

    J flap

29. In which word does *-y* stand for the long *i* sound?

    A apply

    B pretty

    C heavy

    D puppy

30. Which word is the plural of *mess*?

    F messs

    G meses

    H mess

    J messes

31. Which word is a compound word?

    A lipstick

    B crayon

    C spatula

    D creation

32. Which word means "less than zero"?

    F subzero

    G inzero

    H zeroable

    J unzero

33. In which word does *x* stand for the *ks* sounds?

    A examine

    B example

    C ibex

    D exile

Unit 2

In this unit you will learn how to

You will practice the following workplace skills

You will also learn new words and their meanings and put your reading skills to work in written activities. You will get additional reading practice in *Reading Basics Intermediate 1 Reader*.

Lesson 2.1

Identify Sequence

The order in which events take place is called sequence. It is important to know what happens first, second, third, and so on. Look for signal words, such as *first*, *next*, *then*, and *last*. Then you can understand the order in which things happen. You also need to understand sequence in order to follow directions.

When you read, you may find that the writer has put the events in an order different from how they occurred. Look for signal words to help you understand the sequence. Read the example:

> Tahir finished reading the last section of a novel. Before that, he had done the dishes. When he was done with the novel, he made coffee and poured it into the mug he had washed that morning.

Four actions are given in the passage above, but they occurred in an order different from the order in which they are written. Tahir washed a mug, read the last section of a novel, made coffee, and poured it into the clean mug. The words *before that, when he was done,* and *had washed that morning* help the reader understand the order in which things happened.

Sometimes instructions are written as numbered steps. You should follow them in the order in which they are given.

1. Preheat the oven to 350 degrees.
2. Place scoops of cookie dough on an ungreased cookie sheet.
3. Bake cookies for 12 to 14 minutes.
4. Cool for five minutes.
5. Remove cookies from cookie sheet with a spatula.

Circle the signal words in the passage.

> First preheat the oven to 350 degrees. Next place scoops of cookie dough on a cookie sheet. Then bake cookies for 12 to 14 minutes. After that, cool the cookies for five minutes. Finally, remove them from the cookie sheet with a spatula.

Did you circle the words *first, next, then, after that,* and *finally*? Looking for numbers and signal words can help you better understand the sequence of steps in written directions and follow them successfully.

Read the passage. Then circle the letter of the answer to each question.

> The world lost a great pilot when Amelia Earhart's plane vanished in 1937. Earhart was making a trip around the world when her plane went down in the Pacific Ocean. A navy ship picked up a radio message from Earhart. She said she had no fuel. Searchers could not find a trace of her plane. During World War I, Earhart had been a nurse. Then she moved to California and took flying lessons. Soon she bought her own plane. She set a flying record for women. She was the first female passenger to cross the Atlantic Ocean by air. Later she became the first woman pilot to fly across the Atlantic Ocean alone.

1. Which of these events happened first in Amelia Earhart's life?

   A Earhart was a nurse in World War I.

   B Earhart flew across the Atlantic Ocean alone.

   C Earhart took flying lessons.

   D Earhart sent a message to a navy ship.

2. Which event from Amelia Earhart's life took place last?

   F Earhart bought an airplane.

   G Earhart sent a radio message from somewhere in the Pacific Ocean.

   H Earhart set a flying record for women.

   J Earhart flew across the Atlantic Ocean alone.

3. Which event happened in 1937?

   A Earhart set a flying record for women.

   B Earhart's plane vanished.

   C Earhart took flying lessons.

   D Earhart became the first woman passenger to cross the Atlantic Ocean.

4. When did Amelia Earhart buy her own plane?

   F before World War I

   G after 1937

   H before she moved to California

   J after she moved to California

5. What happened after Earhart radioed that she had no fuel?

   A She became the first woman passenger to cross the Atlantic.

   B She became the first woman pilot to fly across the Atlantic Ocean alone.

   C She set a record for flying with no fuel.

   D Searchers could not find her plane.

Read the passage. Then write the steps in the graphic organizer below. Write them in the order in which they happen.

If an inventor wants to obtain a patent for an invention, he or she needs to record the date the invention came to mind. Next he or she should draw a sketch with a description of the idea. Two witnesses should sign the document. Then the inventor submits an application to a patent office. After the form is filed, the patent office checks to make sure that no one else has a patent for the same thing. If the application is accepted, the patent office gives the invention a patent number. This gives the inventor the legal right to the idea for 20 years.

Steps: Obtaining a Patent

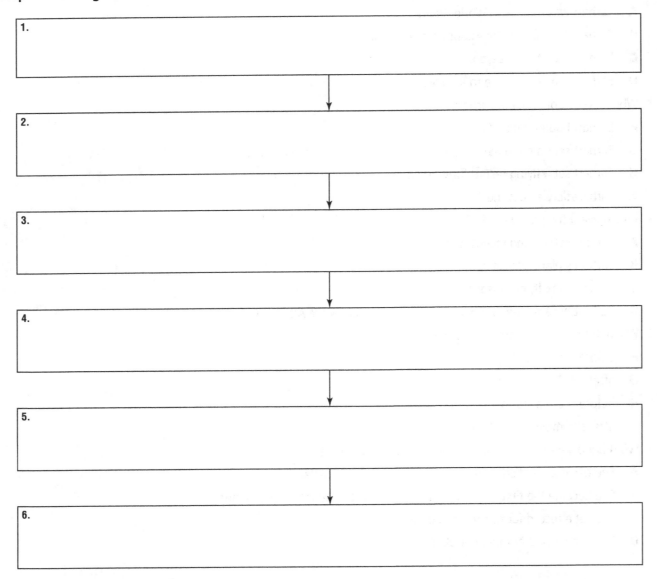

1.

2.

3.

4.

5.

6.

Read the passage. Then circle the letter of the answer to each question.

The fiddler crab changes the color of its skin over the course of each day. Its skin is darkest in the middle of the day, and it lightens as night falls. The fiddler crab adapts its color-changing schedule as the number of daylight hours changes throughout the year. In the winter, when night falls earlier, the fiddler crab gets lighter earlier each evening.

Some scientists wondered what would happen to the fiddler crab in a place where there was no day or night. They put the crab in a laboratory room where they kept the light at a constant level at all times. The crab changed color just as it had on its home beach. It seems that the fiddler crab has a built-in clock that signals the color change. However, the fiddler crab's built-in clock can be reset. When the scientists moved fiddler crabs to a beach in a different time zone, the crabs changed color according to the length of their new day.

1. When is the fiddler crab's skin light?

   A when it is in a laboratory

   B when it is light outside

   C when it is dark outside

   D after its biological clock is reset

2. What happened after the scientists moved the crabs to a beach in a different time zone?

   F The crabs changed color according to the new time zone.

   G The crabs still changed color according to their old time zone.

   H The crabs changed color more slowly.

   J The crabs stopped changing color.

3. What is happening when the crab's skin begins changing color earlier each evening?

   A Spring is beginning.

   B Summer is beginning.

   C The days are getting longer.

   D The days are getting shorter.

4. What did the scientists do before they put crabs in the laboratory?

   F They moved the crabs to a different time zone.

   G They decided the crabs had a built-in clock.

   H They wondered what would happen to the crabs with no day or night.

   J They kept the light at a constant level.

Workplace Skill: Follow a Sequence of Events for a Customer Return

Understanding how to follow step-by-step instructions is important in the workplace. Most companies have procedures for how they want their employees to perform tasks. Employees should try to follow them as closely as possible.

Read the return policy. Then circle the letter of the answer to each question below the box.

Processing a Customer Return

Hill's Department Store prides itself on the quality of its products and the professionalism of its customer-service representatives. When a customer needs to return an item, follow these steps.

1. Be polite and let the customer talk. Many people feel it is necessary to explain why they are returning something. The explanation might not change company policy. However, listening shows the customer that you care.

2. Inspect the item being returned. If the item has parts, open the merchandise. Make sure you have all the pieces. The merchandise must be unused or in new condition.

3. Neatly fold or repack the item in the original packaging.

4. Check that we carry the product at the store. Many times people make the honest mistake of forgetting where an item came from. This happens especially around the holidays. Scan the bar code to check that we sell this product.

5. Have an understanding of the company's policy about returning items:
   - If a customer has a receipt and the item is returned within 30 days of purchase, a full refund is given.
   - After 30 days with a receipt, the store will issue a store credit.
   - Without a receipt, the store will give a store credit for the current price of the merchandise. This price may be less than the customer says he or she paid for the item.

6. Inform the customer of the return options available. Note that there is no way you can change company policy.

1. After listening to the customer explain why he or she is returning an item, what should you do next?

   A run the bar code through the system

   B inspect the item being returned

   C issue a cash refund

   D call your manager for approval

2. If a customer returns an item without a receipt, what can you do?

   F change company policy to issue a full refund

   G be polite and let the customer talk

   H issue a store credit for the current price of the merchandise

   J refuse to give a refund for any reason

Write for Work

When following a sequence of steps, you may find it helpful to put each step in your own words to make sure you understand it. Read the instructions for processing a customer return on page 82. In a notebook, rewrite each numbered step in your own words.

  Reading Extension

Turn to "Mummies" on page 41 of *Reading Basics Intermediate 1 Reader*. After you have read and/or listened to the article, answer the questions below.

Circle the letter of the answer to each question.

1. What step in the mummy-making process was common to Egypt, Peru, Chile, and Italy?

   A They all dried the body thoroughly.

   B They all scooped out the insides.

   C They all put the body in a basket.

   D They all put the body in a catacomb.

2. What did the Egyptians do after they had cleaned out a body?

   F They folded its knees up to its chin.

   G They waited 40 days.

   H They removed the brain.

   J They washed it with wine.

3. Which paragraphs describe the major steps in the process of making a mummy in ancient Egypt?

   A paragraphs 5–7

   B paragraphs 6–11

   C paragraphs 1–5

   D paragraphs 4–9

4. When the people of Peru and Chile made mummies, what did they do after all the liquids were removed from the body?

   F They used salt to completely dry the body.

   G They dressed the body in fancy clothes.

   H They wrapped the body and put it in a basket.

   J The mummies were stretched out flat.

Write the answer to each question.

5. List signal words from the article that helped you understand the order of steps in making a mummy.

   _____

   _____

6. What happened after mummy makers had coated a body with resin?

   _____

   _____

Explore Words

VOWEL COMBINATIONS

When a vowel is followed by a consonant and silent -e, the vowel sound is usually long, as in *cake*, *lime*, and *smoke*. Two vowels can come together and stand for one long vowel sound. Read these vowel combinations that usually stand for long vowel sounds:

Long *a*: *ai, ay*   Long *i*: *ie*   Long *e*: *ea, ee*   Long *u*: *ue*

Read each sentence. Circle the word that has the same vowel sound as the underlined word.

1. If you run, you can <u>make</u> the next train.

2. <u>Pete</u> is coming to visit us next week.

3. These books are due back on <u>June</u> 10.

4. It isn't <u>nice</u> to lie to your kids.

5. I plan to paint the house <u>gray</u>.

6. This is too sweet to <u>eat</u> before lunch.

SYLLABLES

Many words end in a consonant and -le. In words such as *table*, *se<u>ttle</u>*, and *bu<u>bble</u>*, the consonant and -le stay together in the last syllable. The first syllable in consonant + -le words may be open or closed. An open syllable ends in a vowel and has a long vowel sound. A closed syllable ends in a consonant and has a short vowel sound.

Divide each word into syllables. Then write whether the first syllable is open or closed.

1. cradle   _____   _____

2. title   _____   _____

3. sample   _____   _____

4. puzzle   _____   _____

SYNONYMS

Synonyms are words that have the same or almost the same meaning. For example, *odor* and *aroma* are synonyms.

Read each sentence. Circle the letter of the synonym for the underlined word.

1. I try to avoid people I <u>dislike</u>.

    A like

    B enjoy

    C hate

    D know

2. Marco's son gives him a <u>hard</u> time.

    F false

    G difficult

    H easy

    J relaxing

Homophones are words that sound alike but have different spellings and different meanings. For example, *here* and *hear* are homophones. The word *here* means "in this place," while *hear* means "to pick up sound."

Choose the homophone that correctly completes each sentence. Write your answer on the line.

1. I hope I have enough (flour, flower) to make cookies. _____

2. The store is having a (sail, sale) on shoes. _____

3. You can borrow my (jeans, genes) for your date. _____

4. Kids often act up when they are (bored, board). _____

5. We have eaten the (whole, hole) pie. _____

6. He (guest, guessed) what happened at the end of the movie. _____

7. Pia (blew, blue) out the candles on her birthday cake. _____

8. The baseball smashed the window (pain, pane). _____

9. Before you serve the cheese, be sure to remove the (rapper, wrapper). _____

ACADEMIC VOCABULARY

Knowing these high-frequency words will help you in many school subjects.

sequence	the order in which things are connected
obtain	to gain or acquire
section	a part or portion of something
submit	to present to another for review or decision
application	an official request for something

Complete the sentences below using one of the words above.

1. The numbers show the _____ of steps to connect the DVD player.

2. Enriqua filled out the job _____ carefully.

3. What _____ of the newspaper has the main events of the day?

4. He needs to _____ a driver's license to use as an ID.

5. What documents must you _____ in order to get a voter registration card?

Lesson 2.2

Use Supporting Evidence

When writers make a statement or express an opinion in writing, they should support it with evidence. Supporting evidence may be facts, statistics, examples, or reasons.

Good writers include evidence that enhances their arguments. They think carefully about what they are trying to say. Then they include only the evidence that is related to their ideas. A good writer will leave out anything that is unnecessary or contradictory.

It is important for you, as a reader, to evaluate the details in a passage to see if they act as evidence for the main idea, whether it is a fact or an opinion. There may be unrelated details that do not support the main idea. There may also be details that negate or contradict the main idea. You must sort out the details that are not in support of the main idea and then judge whether or not the details that are left are enough to back up the writer's point. Read the example:

> Tito is a dedicated student. He keeps careful track of his assignments and always turns them in on time. He does all of the assigned reading, and he studies even if there is not a test the next day. He loves basketball and follows the Chicago Bulls.

In the passage above, the main idea is stated in the first sentence: "Tito is a dedicated student." The second and third sentences give details that support the main idea. He turns in his assignments on time, and he studies. The last sentence does not support the main idea, but it does not contradict it. Whether Tito likes basketball is unrelated to Tito being a dedicated student. The writer could have left out that detail, but the detail does not weaken the argument.

Read the passage. Underline the detail that supports the boldfaced main idea.

> **Rachel Carson's writings helped make people aware of environmental issues.** She earned a college degree in biology from Pennsylvania College for Women. She wrote conservation bulletins for the government. Her book *Silent Spring* is said to have begun the modern environmental movement. It was published as a book after it was serialized in *The New Yorker.*

Did you underline the sentence, "Her book *Silent Spring* is said to have begun the modern environmental movement"? This is the only detail in the passage that supports the idea that Rachel Carson's writings helped make people aware of environmental issues. The other sentences give details about her background and about the book itself, but they do not support the main idea.

Read each passage. Then circle the letter of the answer to each question.

(1) Exercise has many benefits, and it's never too late to start. (2) My 90-year-old uncle has been lifting weights and walking daily for the past year, and he now looks 10 years younger. (3) If exercise can improve the muscle tone of a 90-year-old man, imagine how good you can look. (4) According to studies, regular workouts also increase metabolism, so people have more energy. (5) I have always had a slow metabolism. (6) Another benefit is that people who exercise sleep better. (7) Finally, since exercise burns calories, you can eat more and not gain weight. (8) Start a new routine today and enjoy the benefits.

1. Which sentence contains the main idea of the text?

   A sentence 1

   B sentence 3

   C sentence 6

   D sentence 8

2. Which sentence does not support the main idea?

   F sentence 2

   G sentence 4

   H sentence 5

   J sentence 8

(1) The auroras are displays of light that fill up the night sky with beautiful colors. (2) Rainbows are beautiful colors in the sky, too. (3) The northern lights are called the aurora borealis. (4) The southern lights are called the aurora australis. (5) The auroras are formed when the sun sends flares of particles into space. (6) Some of the particles loop around Earth's magnetic fields and hit air molecules, causing them to glow. (7) The auroras appear around both the North and South Poles as halos of fire. (8) When the sun is especially active or the solar wind especially strong, the northern lights can be seen much farther south than usual.

3. What is the main idea of this passage?

   A Sun flares can be seen from Earth.

   B There are beautiful light displays at both the North and South Poles.

   C Particles from the sun loop around Earth's magnetic fields.

   D The southern lights are called the aurora australis.

4. Which sentence does not support the main idea?

   F sentence 2

   G sentence 5

   H sentence 6

   J sentence 8

Read each passage and opinion. Then write three pieces of supporting evidence from the passage for each opinion.

Over the years, many offices have adopted a "dress down" practice. Instead of requiring that employees wear suits and ties, employees are free to wear comfortable, casual clothing. Many workers sit in front of computers all day and never interact with customers, so there is no need to dress professionally. Many companies claim that dressing down makes employees happier and more productive.

1. Some offices should not have dress codes.

A _____

_____

B _____

_____

C _____

_____

Some nursing homes have animal therapy programs. People bring dogs to visit nursing home residents. Visiting with a friendly dog for an afternoon has been proven to lower blood pressure and decrease anxiety. Having to care for an animal also makes the sick and elderly feel useful.

2. Nursing homes should have animal therapy programs.

A _____

_____

B _____

_____

C _____

_____

For each statement, circle the letter of the item that supports the opinion.

1. Students should be able to use calculators during their math tests.

   A   It is important to check the answer that a calculator gives to make sure it is correct.

   B   Calculators can help students think through math problems.

   C   Students will stop thinking and become too dependent on machines.

   D   There are different kinds of calculators with many different functions.

2. Wetlands in the United States should be preserved and protected from pollution.

   F   Wetlands are swamps with many poisonous creatures.

   G   Wetlands are ecosystems that protect other ecosystems and help prevent flooding.

   H   Each organism has a different role, or job.

   J   People sometimes change ecosystems to meet their own needs and wants.

3. Everyone should wear a seat belt while in the car.

   A   Passenger fatalities have decreased as seat belt use has increased.

   B   Children should always ride in the backseat.

   C   Sometimes seat belts break, and it is expensive to have them repaired.

   D   It is reasonable to make everyone wear a seat belt even though it is difficult to enforce.

4. There should be a government agency to prevent crime on the Internet.

   F   Government agencies have not proven to be effective in the past.

   G   The Internet has grown too large, too fast.

   H   Many people lose money to Internet crime every week.

   J   Everyone should be guaranteed access to the Internet.

5. People should not send text messages while driving.

   A   Text messaging is an easy way to communicate.

   B   It only takes a few seconds to send a text message.

   C   Crashes occur when people take their eyes off the road to type a text message.

   D   It is safe to type or read a text message when sitting at a stoplight or in traffic.

6. Cell phone use should not be allowed in offices.

   F   Employees may need to make a personal phone call.

   G   Cell phones are small enough to fit in a pocket.

   H   Talking on a cell phone is more professional than texting.

   J   The noise of a cell phone's ring can annoy coworkers.

7. Airlines should reduce the amount of carry-on luggage passengers can bring.

   A   It is difficult to fit everything you need into one suitcase.

   B   With the current allowance, the overhead compartment always fills up before everyone has boarded.

   C   There is not a lot of leg room between seats.

   D   It takes a long time for passengers to claim their checked baggage.

Workplace Skill: Find Supporting Details in a Project Start-up Procedure

In order to understand a business document, you must be able to recognize the facts, examples, and details that support the main idea. Many companies have standard procedures for how certain projects should be handled. These procedures help employees know who is in charge at any given point in a project—from beginning to end.

Read the passage. Then circle the letter of the answer to each question below the box.

Project Start-up to Close-out Procedures

Project Code: When a project is awarded and work is to begin, a project code is required. The Vice President of Finance creates a project code and informs key departments and personnel what it is. Project employees are to use this code on all time sheets, expense reports, and billing requests.

Budget Meeting: The Vice President of Finance then schedules an initial budget meeting with all department managers. Monthly budget meetings will also take place to review ongoing projects.

Launch Meeting: Once a project code is issued, the Production Project Manager will schedule a launch meeting to start the project. All key department personnel involved in the project will attend. The assigned Production Project Manager will host the launch meeting.

Ongoing Meetings: The Production Project Manager is responsible for sending electronic invitations for every meeting to all key personnel. He or she is responsible for leading the meetings and creating and distributing an Open Issues Log. The Open Issues Log keeps track of unfinished components of the project and who is responsible for them. This log is distributed at all meetings.

Close-out: Final invoices and a wrap-up meeting will trigger the final close-out phase. Each department involved will have specific close-out checklists to complete.

1. What is the first thing needed to begin work on a project?

   A   a launch meeting

   B   a project code

   C   a budget meeting

   D   a final invoice

2. If you are the Vice President of Finance for this company, what is one of your responsibilities?

   F   to send electronic invititations for all meetings

   G   to create an Open Issues Log

   H   to provide lunch at meetings

   J   to create a project code and inform all key personnel what it is

Write for Work

Imagine you are a member of one of the key departments involved in the project start-up. Read the procedures on page 90. In a notebook, write the main idea of the procedures. Write three details from the procedures that support the main idea.

 Reading Extension

Turn to "Escape from Iran" on page 49 of *Reading Basics Intermediate 1 Reader*. After you have read and/or listened to the article, answer the questions below.

Circle the letter of the answer to each question.

1. The author says that Americans thought the Canadians were heroes. What evidence supports this?

   A Americans sent thank-you letters to the Canadian government.

   B Some American musicians wrote a song about the Canadian heroes.

   C The Iranian outrage was aimed at Canada.

   D No one knew that the CIA had also helped get the Americans out.

2. In paragraph 13, the author says that the Americans were in great danger. What evidence from the article supports this?

   F Mendez's plan wasn't working fast enough.

   G Taylor sent many Canadian staff members on unnecessary trips.

   H Mendez's script was not believable as a science-fiction thriller.

   J A phone call proved that the Iranians knew where some Americans were hiding.

3. In paragraph 18, the author says that the Iranians were furious at the Canadians. What evidence from the article supports this?

   A The Iranians never gave them a second look.

   B The Iranians flew Canadian flags next to American ones.

   C The Iranians issued threats against Canada.

   D The Iranians stormed the U.S. Embassy.

Write the answer to each question.

4. Why were the Iranians angry at Canada?

   _____

5. What details did Mendez create to make his film company believable?

   _____

   _____

Explore Words

When a vowel or vowel pair is followed by the letter *r*, the vowel stands for an unexpected sound. For example, say these word pairs: *mat / mart*, *spot / sport*, *shot / short*, *head / heard*. The second word in each pair has an *r*-controlled vowel sound.

Read each row of words. Circle the word that has an *r*-controlled vowel sound.

1. crab	curb	club	class	create	cringe
2. skinny	skate	scant	scratch	scope	scar
3. change	challenge	chilly	charge	chain	cheek
4. skirt	skill	school	skunk	scale	scoop
5. shot	shown	shops	shock	should	short
6. movie	mango	means	market	mined	mails

SYLLABLES

A syllable is a word part that has one vowel sound. An open syllable ends in a vowel and usually has a long vowel sound. A closed syllable ends in a consonant and usually has a short vowel sound. Many words have two vowels separated by two consonants. Divide those words between the two consonants. Other words end in a consonant and *-le*. The consonant and *-le* usually stay together in the last syllable.

Divide each word into syllables. Then write whether the first syllable is open or closed. The first item has been done for you.

1. absent   *ab / sent*   *closed*   **4.** candle   _____ _____

2. stable   _____ _____   **5.** insect   _____ _____

3. gossip   _____ _____   **6.** maple   _____ _____

ANTONYMS

Antonyms are words that have the opposite or almost the opposite meaning. For example, *beautiful* and *ugly* are antonyms.

Circle the antonyms in each numbered row.

1. strong	deep	shallow	mighty	**4.** smooth	sweet	rough	pale
2. easy	plain	hard	possible	**5.** polite	stupid	smart	student
3. ill	dead	gone	alive	**6.** shy	cruel	selfish	kind

COMPOUND WORDS

Compound words are words that are made up of two words. You can often use the meanings of the two words to figure out the meaning of a compound word. For example, the word *storeroom* is a compound word. It is made up of the words *store* and *room*. A storeroom is a room where things are stored.

Match a word from the first column with a word from the second column. Write the letter on the line. Then write the word.

_____ **1.** fire	**a.** bag	_____
_____ **2.** bee	**b.** style	_____
_____ **3.** book	**c.** fighter	_____
_____ **4.** card	**d.** quake	_____
_____ **5.** count	**e.** sauce	_____
_____ **6.** apple	**f.** hive	_____
_____ **7.** hair	**g.** down	_____
_____ **8.** earth	**h.** board	_____

ACADEMIC VOCABULARY

Knowing these high-frequency words will help you in many school subjects.

judge to form a conclusion

support to give assistance to

include to make part of a whole or set

enhance to increase or improve the quality or value of

argument a set of reasons given with the goal of persuading others

Complete the sentences below using one of the words above.

1. The audience had to _____ which cupcakes were the best.

2. Marissa made sure to _____ both a map and a set of written directions to the dinner.

3. As he spoke, Jacobo made many good points in his _____.

4. Kareem's family needed to _____ him during the difficult times.

5. She used cosmetics to _____ her natural beauty.

Lesson 2.3

Identify Style Techniques

INTRODUCE

A writer's style is his or her own way of saying things. Style refers to the way an author uses words, sentence structure, and language to communicate ideas. The words that are used, the types of sentences, and even the punctuation should all work together. Style can reveal a writer's attitude or purpose for writing.

Writing styles can be informal or formal, flowery or simple, dramatic or straightforward. An informal style is like a conversation, with slang words and incomplete sentences. A formal style generally uses more difficult words and longer sentences. Flowery writing usually has many descriptive words and long, flowing sentences.

Writers use a variety of techniques to express their ideas. Some writers include many descriptive details to help the reader picture people, places, or events. Others use dialogue to develop a scene. Writers also use punctuation in interesting ways. For example, a writer might use a dash (—) for emphasis or to show excitement. Read these examples:

> Monifa leaned in close to the fluttering moths as they jostled for space around the flickering light. Never had she seen such variety—or numbers!

> Monifa set up her lantern and lit the wick. Hundreds of moths rushed toward the light. Monifa leaned in close to observe them.

The opening sentence in the first example is long and descriptive, with the words *fluttering, jostled,* and *flickering.* The dash and exclamation point in the next sentence help to convey Monifa's excitement. The second example is more straightforward, and the shorter sentences highlight the action.

Read the passage. Then decide what style techniques the writer has used.

> With each step up the ladder, Vicari felt the cold pit in his stomach growing. His hands were tingling. The hair on the back of his neck stood up. At one point, he glanced down. The water looked cold and steely. It seemed so far away. Could he keep going? At last, he reached the diving board.

The writer of this passage uses descriptive language and details to communicate Vicari's fear of diving off the board. The short, choppy sentences add to the feeling of fear.

Read the description of each writer's style. Then read each passage. Write the label for the writer who most likely wrote the passage.

Writer A uses long, flowing sentences to describe actions.

Writer B uses highly descriptive language that paints effective word pictures.

Writer C uses dialogue extensively to reveal character traits and feelings.

Writer D uses punctuation for explanation and emphasis.

> Lena's gown fit her perfectly. She seemed to float down the stairs in a cloud of airy pink mist. Her glistening hair was swept up elegantly and held by a delicate silver clasp. Her skin glowed with health and the excitement of her first formal dance.

1. _____

> "This is an easy trek." I kept reassuring my little brother as we followed the trail, but he wouldn't stop complaining.
>
> "The path is slippery, and I would've tripped if I hadn't held onto the branch of that tree," he complained.
>
> "We're halfway there—you don't want to go back," I called to him.
>
> "It's getting muddier and muddier, and I want to turn around," he insisted.
>
> "Be sure to watch your step on these logs," I shouted back. Then turning my head to make sure he had heard, I slipped into a creek in what felt like slow motion. My brother soon caught up with me, laughing for the first time all day.

2. _____

> The week before the concert, Kenji practiced his solo piece every evening. And each day, at work, he found his fingers playing the computer keys as though he were still at the piano. At night, the music played over and over in his mind as he tried to sleep. Even after all this practice, he still did not feel ready on the day of the concert. As he climbed the stairs to the stage, his legs trembled uncontrollably. How was he going to be able to play? To his surprise, when he approached the gleaming piano, he felt that the music was there—waiting for him to share it.

3. _____

Read each passage. Identify which style technique listed in the box was used. Some
passages may use more than one style technique.

long sentences	dialogue	punctuation for emphasis
descriptive details	action	

Imagine a sea animal that looks a lot like a pincushion with a great many pins
sticking straight out. This is the sea urchin—a small, round creature covered with
spines. The spines are used both for protection and for locomotion. A sea urchin's
spines are barbed, like fishhooks. This makes them very difficult to remove once
they are embedded in the skin. The spines are very brittle, so they break off easily
from the urchin. Some sea urchins also have a poison in their spines, which causes
a painful sting.

1. _____

A city dog journeyed to the country to visit a farm dog. All of the country dogs
were afraid of a small black animal with a white stripe down its back.

"You're all wimps!" the city dog exclaimed. "I can beat you and your friends and
the striped animal, too. Lead me to him immediately!"

The farm dog calmly responded, "This is a brand new world for you. Don't you
want to ask questions about this little animal first?"

2. _____

With a sigh of relief, Biyen got behind his steering wheel for the four-hour drive
home. Biyen was wide awake for the first hour of his trip. Then he stopped for a
cup of coffee and figured he'd be fine. For the next hour, he kept the window wide
open and welcomed the bite of the frosty air. Then he began singing loudly to
himself. Suddenly, a siren got his attention—and woke him up! An attentive state
trooper had noticed Biyen's car swerving on the highway and was pulling him over.
The ticket was one he would be glad to pay.

3. _____

Read each passage. Circle the letter of the style technique used in each passage.

Carlos heard terrible screams coming from down the hall. "There's a bat!" Anita yelled as she ran into the bedroom and dove under the covers. Carlos slammed the door just in time to keep out the tiny creature with the enormous flapping black wings. Anita clutched the blanket around her as Carlos dialed the number for animal control.

1. A short sentences   **C** punctuation for emphasis

    B action   **D** dialogue

This city has a fantastic commuter rail system—probably the best one in the country! It's easy, simple really, to use. The first thing you need to do is to get to the right station—it's up to you to make your way there. Then you need a special commuter rail ticket. You can't use your prepaid card (I don't know why), so you'll need to buy a ticket at the window. Then wait for your train at the platform. Make sure you're on time—the trains are never late!

2. F dialogue   **H** short sentences

    G action   **J** punctuation for emphasis

Tai finally made it over the ridge. The land flattened out here, and the river got wider and shallower. Dozens of people were wading in the water with their children and dogs. The children shrieked as the dogs shook out their damp fur, sending drops of water flying. Tai kept walking, and after half a mile, she reached the waterfall. The cool spray of the water refreshed her as it misted over her hot, sweaty face.

3. A description   **C** informal language

    B dialogue   **D** short sentences

Katya searched through the racks of dresses, pushing each hanger forward in frustration. She needed a new dress, and she needed it right away. When she had gotten the invitation to the banquet, she hadn't realized how difficult it would be to find a dress that was fancy enough. Discouraged, she walked out and made her way to the next store on her list.

4. F long sentences   **H** description

    G dialogue   **J** punctuation for emphasis

Workplace Skill:
Identify Style Techniques in E-mails

Business documents reflect different styles depending on the type of correspondence. Most business communications, such as memos, letters, and policies, are written in a formal style. The writers often use long, complex sentences. The tone is serious and professional. Other business correspondence, such as internal e-mails, can use casual, informal language. They can include slang, abbreviations, and contractions.

Read the e-mails. Then circle the letter of the answer to each question below the boxes.

From: Raymond Silva
To: curtisowen@VTNmarketing.com
Subject: Benton Deal

Hi, Curtis,

Listen, I think I can close the Benton deal! He's really more interested in promise than price. Wanted to hear what we could offer his company in the future. So, Curt, I scribbled some notes about our past performance. Then I threw in comments about our planned improvements for next year. I feel better knowing I won't have to walk into our next meeting cold. I'll have facts at my fingertips. It should be a done deal!

From: raymondsilva@VTNmarketing.com
To: Christopher_Benton@xzgraphics.com
Subject: Marketing Campaign

Dear Mr. Benton:

I want to take this opportunity to thank you for taking the time to meet with me yesterday. We are very eager to be the company you select for your new marketing campaign. I have taken the time to compose a list of our past successful marketing campaigns. I have also prepared an outline on how our proposal would lead to success. I would like to meet with you next week at a time that is convenient for you.

---

1. Which is the most likely reason the writer wrote the second e-mail in a formal style?

   A He wants to sound casual.

   B He wants to sound professional.

   C He is writing to a coworker.

   D He has met Mr. Benton on several occasions.

2. What is one element that identifies the first e-mail as informal writing?

   F the use of longer, more complex sentences

   G the lack of contractions

   H the avoidance of slang and everyday language

   J the use of slang and incomplete sentences

Write for Work

Imagine you have just met with the friend of a relative who has decided to recommend you for a job interview at her company. You plan to send a thank-you letter or e-mail to this person for meeting with you. Decide whether you should use a formal or informal writing style. In your notebook, write a draft of the letter.

 Reading Extension

Turn to "Alone at Sea" on page 57 of *Reading Basics Intermediate 1 Reader*. After you have read and/or listened to the article, answer the questions below.

Circle the letter of the answer to each question.

1. Reread paragraph 1. Which style technique is used in this paragraph?

   A   short sentences

   B   action

   C   description

   D   long sentences

2. Reread paragraph 4. Which style technique is used in this paragraph?

   F   dialogue

   G   action

   H   punctuation for emphasis

   J   long sentences

3. Reread paragraph 13. Which style technique is used to convey loneliness?

   A   description

   B   action

   C   punctuation for emphasis

   D   long sentences

4. Reread paragraph 14. Which style technique is used in this paragraph?

   F   short sentences

   G   action

   H   description

   J   long sentences

Write the answer to the question.

5. Rewrite paragraph 18, using one of the following style techniques: dialogue, action, description, or long sentences.

   _____

   _____

   _____

   _____

Explore Words

VOWEL COMBINATIONS

Some vowel combinations stand for the long vowel sound of the first letter in the pair. In each word below, a vowel combination stands for the long vowel sound shown.

Long *o*:	soap	toe	thr<u>ow</u>
Long *i*:	t<u>ie</u>	cr<u>ie</u>s	
Long *u*:	arg<u>ue</u>	bl<u>ue</u>	

Read each word aloud. Circle the word if it has a long *o* sound. Underline the word once if it has a long *u* sound and twice if it has a long *i* sound. The first item has been done for you.

1. (roast)
2. flies
3. goes

4. rescue
5. crow
6. true

7. died
8. value
9. cloak

SPELLING: HOMOPHONES

Homophones are words that sound alike but are spelled differently and have different meanings. *Some* and *sum* are homophones. *Some* means "a few." *Sum* means "total."

Circle the word that correctly completes each sentence.

1. Have you ever ridden on a (hoarse, horse)?
2. I (would, wood) really like to visit a guest ranch.
3. Prashanti's kids are not (aloud, allowed) to watch TV.

4. Do you know who (won, one) today's game?
5. My family tries not to (waist, waste) food.
6. It is very rude to (stare, stair) at people.

SPELLING: WORD ENDINGS

You can add word endings such as *-ed, -ing, -er,* and *-est* onto many base words. Sometimes, you have to change the spelling of a base word when you add an ending. If a word ends in silent *-e,* drop the *e.* Then add the ending: *bake / baked / baking.* If a word ends with a consonant that comes after one vowel, double the consonant. Then add the ending: *sad / sadder / saddest.*

Add an ending to each word. Write the new word on the line.

1. attend + ing _____
2. strong + est _____
3. scare + ed _____

4. dig + ing _____
5. erase + er _____
6. zigzag + ed _____

SYLLABLES

Every word has one or more syllables. A closed syllable ends with a consonant and usually has a short vowel sound. An open syllable ends with a vowel and usually has a long vowel sound. When a vowel is followed by one consonant, first try dividing after the vowel and pronounce the syllables. For example, divide *river: ri / ver*. When the word is divided that way, the first syllable is open and usually has a long *i* sound. That doesn't sound like a familiar word. Now divide after the consonant: *riv / er*. Now the first syllable is closed and has a short *i* sound. The word sounds correct.

Divide each word into syllables. Then write whether the first syllable is open or closed. The first item has been done for you.

1. wagon *wag / on* *closed*

2. pilot _____ _____

3. crazy _____ _____

4. cabin _____ _____

5. program _____ _____

6. comet _____ _____

7. robin _____ _____

8. carton _____ _____

9. salad _____ _____

10. melon _____ _____

11. labor _____ _____

12. below _____ _____

13. pilgrim _____ _____

14. broken _____ _____

ACADEMIC VOCABULARY

Knowing these high-frequency words will help you in many school subjects.

style	a way of using language
communicate	to express or transmit information
technique	a way of doing things
emphasis	special importance given to something
highlight	to draw attention to

Complete the sentences below using one of the words above.

1. In her painting class, Marietta learned a new _____ for creating shadows.

2. Luisa made sure to _____ the most important points in the text as she studied.

3. When Apera learned to _____ better, he found he was able to get better jobs.

4. The fitness instructor really placed a lot of _____ on using correct body form.

5. The writer's _____ was short and choppy.

Lesson 2.4

Make Generalizations

When you read, it is helpful to be able to recognize and make generalizations. A generalization is a general statement that is applied to many people, events, or situations. To identify generalizations, look for these signal words: *all, most, many, few, usually, generally,* and *typically.* You might be able to recognize a generalization by signal words, but not all generalizations use these words.

To make a generalization, think about facts or specific examples that lead you to draw a logical conclusion. For example, suppose that you meet many people who have dogs, and all those people are friendly. You might make this generalization: *All dog owners are friendly.* However, be careful—there are certainly some dog owners who are *not* friendly. A better generalization would be: <u>*Many*</u> *dog owners are friendly.* Read the example:

> At dog parks, owners can let their dogs run and play without leashes. Some dogs bound around the grass, happy to run free. Some dogs enjoy playing with new people and new dogs. Most dogs love to spend time at the dog park.

The last sentence in the example is a generalization about many dogs. *Most* is the signal word. The sentences that come before it give specific examples of how dogs enjoy themselves at the dog park, and the last sentence makes a generalization based on the examples.

You must be careful that the generalizations you make are valid. A valid generalization is based on a number of specific examples. The more examples you consider in order to make a generalization, the more likely it is to be valid. If you base your generalization on too few examples, or if you interpret your examples incorrectly, your generalization will be invalid.

Read the passage and decide what logical generalization you can make.

> Insects are good sources of protein. Some people in South Africa roast termites and eat them like popcorn. Many people in the United States eat fried caterpillars and chocolate-covered ants and bees. Several African groups enjoy boiled locusts. They even use the locust legs, which they grind and mix with peanut butter.

Did you generalize that many people around the world eat insects? That statement makes sense and is supported by information in the passage.

Read each passage. Then circle the letter of the answer to each question.

> An elephant uses its trunk to smell the air. It also uses its trunk to carry food and water to its mouth. It can even give itself a shower by shooting a stream of water from its trunk. The elephant can lift heavy loads by wrapping its trunk around them. The sensitive tip of an elephant's trunk lets the animal pick up objects as small as a coin. Finally, the elephant uses its trunk to caress its young.

1. From this passage, one can generalize that an elephant's trunk

  A is amazingly strong and useful.

  B grows rapidly after the elephant is born.

  C is easily injured.

  D often gets in its way.

> Elephants stay close to each other in herds in order to defend each other if the herd is attacked. The adult elephants make a circle around the young ones to protect them. If one elephant is injured, another will try to rescue it and nudge it to safety. Most animals have no problem leaving the weak behind to die, but elephants are distressed by such situations. They mourn and grieve for very long periods of time.

2. From this passage, one can generalize that elephants

  F usually attack other animals for no reason.

  G are very loyal to fellow herd members.

  H leave their herd when they are fully grown.

  J spend all of their time defending the herd.

> Fish live in the ocean, as well as in rivers, lakes, ponds, and streams. Some live close to the surface, and others live near the bottom of the sea. Most fish have streamlined bodies and fins that help them move easily through the water. They also have gills that take in oxygen from water. Some bony fish have a special gas-filled swim bladder that helps them adjust their swimming depth.

3. From this passage, one can generalize that fish

  A are a good source of protein.

  B move very quickly through the water.

  C are easy to tame and keep as pets.

  D adapt to different environments.

Read each passage. Then complete the sentence with a logical generalization that is based on the passage.

Alessandro plays on the high school soccer team every autumn. In winter and spring, he plays on a club team, and he attends at least two soccer camps during the summer. Alessandro subscribes to three soccer magazines. The walls of his room are covered with posters of his favorite professional soccer players.

1. From this passage, I can generalize that Alessandro always

_____

The Khouris' dog Tuffy eats premium dog food every day. Tuffy has a healthy, shiny coat and bright eyes. He enjoys playing and going for walks with the family for an hour every afternoon. He has lots of energy and is relaxed with people.

2. From this passage, I can generalize that Tuffy's owners usually

_____

The radio station WZIG plays oldies from the 1960s, 1970s, and 1980s. WZIG airs advertisements for investment companies and retirement communities. The station holds contests about political trivia. The prizes are often expensive trips or cruises. Most of the DJs are men and women in their 50s.

3. From this passage, I can generalize that most of the WZIG listeners

_____

Tameeka belongs to a book club at the public library and reads three or four books a month. Members meet every three weeks to discuss a novel they have read. Tameeka takes a book along with her on the train so that she can read on the way to and from work. She also reads during her lunch break.

4. From this passage, I can generalize that when Tameeka has free time, she usually

_____

Read each passage. Then circle the letter of the answer that completes each sentence.

> Malia has three cats, two dogs, and a parakeet at home. She volunteers at the animal shelter one day each week. There she helps care for animals that have been abandoned. Malia also supports a local wildlife refuge shelter, which cares for injured and orphaned wild animals.

1. From this passage you can generalize that Malia
   A has a job working with animals.
   B never has time to spend with human friends.
   C likes to care for animals in need.
   D had no pets when she was growing up.

> Hamid will not walk under a ladder. If he steps on a crack in the sidewalk, he throws salt over his shoulder. Hamid avoids black cats, and he has no mirrors on the walls of his house. He is afraid he might break one, and that would mean seven years of bad luck.

2. From this passage you can generalize that Hamid
   F is superstitious.
   G is afraid of cats.
   H has a great sense of humor.
   J has no ladders in his home.

> Two musical groups held concerts at the Muldoon Center in Springfield last month. The city's pro basketball and hockey teams play their home games at the Muldoon Center. Conventions can book the center for large group meetings.

3. From this passage, you can generalize that when people need a big meeting center in Springfield
   A they frequently use the Muldoon Center.
   B they have to find a place in another town.
   C the Muldoon Center is too far away.
   D the Muldoon Center is too expensive for most of them.

Workplace Skill:
Make Generalizations from a Salary Table

Tables and charts are useful documents in the workplace. Because data are placed in columns and rows, it is easy to compare and contrast information and make generalizations. It is helpful to have facts or specific examples when making logical generalizations.

Read the salary table. Then circle the letter of the answer to each question below the box.

Computer Science Teachers Comparison of Wage Distribution by Metropolitan Areas 2009*

Location	Pay Period	10th percentile	25th percentile	Median	75th percentile	90th percentile
United States	Yearly	$37,000	$51,000	$68,600	$94,700	$125,700
Los Angeles, CA Metropolitan Div.	Yearly	$43,900	$58,900	$80,200	$109,200	$148,200
Bethesda, MD Metropolitan Div.	Yearly	$46,400	$61,900	$79,200	$97,700	$125,500
Boston, MA NECTA Div.	Yearly	$42,800	$70,700	$101,500	$127,700	$154,000

* Note: Where an individual should expect to fall in a wage distribution is not always an easy judgment. Those who are just starting their careers may expect wages at the lower end of the distribution, near the 10th or 25th percentile. Those with more experience and education may expect wages near the 75th or 90th percentile. *Median* is the number in the middle of a set of numbers arranged from smallest to largest.

1. Why would it be difficult to determine the exact wage rate for a particular computer science teacher in Chicago, IL?

   A Most computer science teachers have the same level of education.

   B There is no wage distribution data available for computer science teachers in Chicago.

   C Levels of experience and education vary with each individual.

   D Most computer science teachers fall within the 90th percentile.

2. From this table, one can generalize that most beginning computer science teachers in Bethesda, MD,

   F have less experience than teachers in Los Angeles.

   G are paid more than teachers in Boston.

   H are paid more than teachers in many other places.

   J have the same education levels as teachers in Boston.

Write for Work

Suppose you are a career counselor for a teacher resource center. You have been asked by the center to study the table on page 106. They would like you to make two or three generalizations based on the data in the table. Write your generalizations in a notebook.

 Reading Extension

Turn to "Night Killers" on page 65 of *Reading Basics Intermediate 1 Reader*. After you have read and/or listened to the article, answer the questions below.

Circle the letter of the answer to each question.

1. Based on the article, which of the following statements is a logical generalization?
   - **A** All people who live in Central America should eat garlic.
   - **B** Most vampire bats prefer human blood to animal blood.
   - **C** All vampire bats drink blood.
   - **D** Vampire bats endanger people throughout the world.

2. Based on the article, which of the following statements is NOT a logical generalization?
   - **F** Vampire bats are most dangerous to humans after storms.
   - **G** Garlic is a short-term deterrent against vampire bats.
   - **H** Being a vampire-bat killer is a dangerous job.
   - **J** Most vampire bats are killed by sunlight.

3. Reread paragraph 5. What generalization can you make about rabies?
   - **A** Rabies is an extremely serious disease.
   - **B** Rabies only affects cows.
   - **C** Rabies is not that serious.
   - **D** There is an available cure for rabies.

Write the answer to the question.

4. Suppose you were telling someone about the information in this article. What generalization about vampire bats would you make?

_____

_____

_____

Explore Words

HARD AND SOFT c AND g

The letters *c* and *g* each stand for two sounds. Hard *c* sounds the same as the letter *k*, as in *castle* and *cave*. Soft *c* sounds the same as the letter *s*, as in *city* and *cent*. Hard *g* is the sound you hear at the beginning of *gold*. Soft *g* sounds the same as the letter *j*, as in *giant*.

Read the words. Write *hard* or *soft* on the line to show the sound of the underlined letter in each word.

1. <u>c</u>aptain _____

2. dan<u>c</u>e _____

3. <u>g</u>allon _____

4. ra<u>g</u>e _____

5. <u>c</u>ash _____

6. gara<u>g</u>e _____

CONSONANT PAIRS kn, wr, gn

Some consonant pairs include one silent letter. In *kn, wr,* and *gn,* the first letter in each pair is silent, as in <u>kn</u>ock, <u>wr</u>eck, and si<u>gn</u>.

Write *kn, wr,* or *gn* on the line to complete each word.

1. _____ife

2. _____at

3. _____ee

4. desi_____

5. _____eath

6. _____ist

7. _____ock

8. _____ow

9. _____ew

10. _____ote

11. _____ong

12. si_____ed

PREFIXES pre-, pro-

A prefix is a word part that can be added to the beginning of words. Prefixes change the meanings of words to which they are added. For example, the prefix *pre-* means "before" or "earlier." The prefix *pro-* means "in support of." *Pregame* means "before the game," and *prowar* means "in support of war."

Read the sentences. Write the meaning of each underlined word on the line.

1. The woman bought a <u>preshrunk</u> blouse. _____

2. The <u>prolabor</u> workers went on strike. _____

3. Atian had to <u>preheat</u> the oven before putting in the roast. _____

4. The protesters are <u>prodemocracy</u>. _____

SPELLING: POSSESSIVES

Possessive words show that something belongs to one person or more than one person. Singular possessive words always include an apostrophe followed by s ('s). For example, the CDs that belong to one girl are *the girl's CDs*. Plural possessive words usually include an s followed by an apostrophe (s'). For example, the CDs that belong to several girls are *the girls' CDs*.

Rewrite each phrase with 's or s' to show ownership. The first item has been done for you.

1. the pictures that belong to his parents   *his parents' pictures*

2. the patients that belong to the doctor   _____

3. the lunches that belong to the workers   _____

4. the car that belongs to my brother   _____

5. the children that belong to my sisters   _____

6. the tools that belong to the carpenter   _____

7. the fleas that live on the dogs   _____

8. the support we get from our families   _____

ACADEMIC VOCABULARY

Knowing these high-frequency words will help you in many school subjects.

general   broad, not specific

applies   has to do with

events   happenings

specific   exact or definite

logical   clearly and soundly reasoned

Complete the sentences below using one of the words above.

1. If you write _____ on the calendar, you won't forget them.

2. Math is easy because the rules are _____.

3. This rule _____ to everyone.

4. Please be _____ when you tell me what to do.

5. I can give you a _____ idea of when I'll be there but not an exact time.

Lesson 2.5

Recognize Author's Purpose, Effect, and Intention

Everything you read is written for a reason. That reason is the author's purpose. Identifying the author's purpose will help you better understand the meaning of the passage. The most common purposes for writing are to persuade, to inform, to explain, to entertain, and to describe.

Read the example. The author's purpose is to persuade.

> Cigarettes kill. Studies show that about 85 percent of all lung cancer deaths are directly caused by smoking. If you smoke, stop. If you don't smoke, don't start.

In this example, the author wants to persuade people to avoid smoking. To accomplish his or her purpose, an author must decide on an approach toward the material and audience. This author has used style techniques—the choice of strong words, the use of direct address, and a short punchy sentence—to create an effect of seriousness, or warning. This effect reveals that the author's intention is to convey the serious nature of the problem of smoking.

An author's style can also create such effects as excitement, suspense, or humor. Each of these effects reveals the author's intention.

Read the passage and identify the author's purpose, effect, and intention.

> Welcome to the company! We are happy that you have joined our team. Your daily responsibilities as our receptionist are quite straightforward. First, when you arrive, check your voice mail for messages. If someone has called in sick, please let our office manager know right away. Your second priority is to check e-mail and pass on any questions. If it isn't clear to whom the question should go, don't be afraid to ask for help. We all remember what it was like to be new. Throughout the day, you will be receiving phone calls and e-mails. At the end of each day, check the supplies and list anything that's running low on an order sheet. If a staff member needs something important, fax the order sheet to Office Works right away. Otherwise, all orders can be sent together on Friday.

The purpose of the passage is to inform a new receptionist about his or her responsibilities. The language and style of the passage create a welcoming effect. It is clear that the author's intention is to provide information in a way that makes the new receptionist feel comfortable.

Read each passage. Then answer the questions.

Extending the bike path would benefit the environment, the community, and our local economy. First, a landscaped path would improve air quality since plants remove carbon dioxide from the atmosphere. Second, a path would make it easier for children and adults to exercise. They could also ride bikes more safely. Finally, new stores might open up along the path to provide food and cold drinks. Please help us raise funds for this important project.

1. What is the author's purpose? _____

2. How does the author convey the importance of the issue? What words show this?

_____

The storm clouds gathered as Miguel and Sonrisa listened to the news on the car's radio. They heard the wind howling outside. Already there were reports of trees down and flooded highways. People were advised by the police to leave town using Highway 601 rather than the local roads. Miguel stopped and put the car in reverse when he saw a power line lying in the street. Suddenly, Miguel and Sonrisa heard a loud clap of thunder, and a large object hit the roof of the car.

3. What is the author's purpose? _____

4. Does the author's writing style create an effect of suspense or humor?

_____

I cringed and squirmed as I sank lower into the dentist's chair. With every poke, prod, and scrape, I wished I had brushed and flossed more often. "A little more plaque than there ought to be here," said Dr. Gunnar. "Uhhhhhh," I groaned. I was miserable because I knew I had only brought this on myself. I will brush three times a day, floss once a day, and never eat between meals, I thought. As I left, I chanted this mantra to myself. I promised myself that next time my teeth will be sparkling.

5. What is the author's purpose? _____

6. Is the author's intention to create suspense or to express mixed feelings?

_____

Read each passage. Then answer the questions below.

> What creature has a head like a horse, a tail like a monkey, and a pouch like a kangaroo? I'm sure you can guess if you think hard enough. It's the sea horse, of course! Despite its name, a sea horse is not really a horse. It is a funny little fish that travels in an upright position. Sea horses spend a lot of time with their flexible tails wrapped around plants.

1. What is the author's purpose?

_____

2. What is the author's intention?

_____

3. What clues in the text help you to determine the author's intention?

_____

_____

> City council members, please take note. The stop sign at the corner of Linden Street and Rolfe Road has become very dangerous to both drivers and pedestrians. Many accidents occur at this corner, and it is only a matter of time before someone is fatally hurt. Drivers proceeding along Linden often fail to obey the stop sign because they wrongly assume that traffic coming from the left is going to turn right. The immediate installation of a traffic light at this intersection would greatly reduce the risk of injury to drivers.

4. What is the author's purpose?

_____

5. Does the writing convey a sense that the issue is critical or trivial?

_____

6. Which words and phrases help to create this effect?

_____

Read each passage. Then circle the letter of the answer to each question.

> As we headed out the driveway for our vacation, the windshield wiper broke and flapped against the glass with each swipe. Things only got worse. The first night, we couldn't find a motel room. It seems there was a fishing derby going on in the region. I don't know if rain makes for good fishing, but I felt sorry for all of the people fishing in the downpour. Still, I didn't feel *that* sorry because all the motel rooms for miles were full of fishers and their families. We finally found a run-down place after midnight. There were cigarette burns in the carpet and a water stain on the bathroom ceiling. I slept with my clothes on and vowed to plan ahead next year.

1. What is the author's main purpose in this passage?

    A to persuade others to plan their vacations ahead of time

    B to persuade motels not to give all of their rooms to fishers

    C to tell a story about a vacation

    D to tell a story about a fishing derby

2. Based on the passage, what do you think the author's intention was for writing?

    F to describe the joys of car travel

    G to caution readers about staying in motels

    H to entertain with a funny story

    J to influence fishing derby organizers to reschedule their derbies

> There should be a picture of a toad beside the word *ugly* in the dictionary. It is surely one of the ugliest creatures on Earth. Its rough skin is covered with warts, knobs, and creases. Its middle is fat, and its legs are squatty. Its eyes never blink, and they stick up like lamps above the long, grim slash of its mouth.

3. What is the author's main purpose in this passage?

    A to explain something ugly

    B to explain something beautiful

    C to tell a story about studying toads

    D to tell a scary story about seeing an ugly toad

4. What effect does the language help to create?

    F a feeling of suspense

    G a feeling of excitement

    H a feeling of humor

    J a feeling of anger

Workplace Skill: Understand Author's Purpose in an Employee Memo

Employers use memos to give information about their company plans and policies. They also use memos to describe company procedures. Memos always have a specific purpose. A memo should have the name of the sender and the name of the recipient or recipients. It should also include the subject and the date.

Read the memo. Then circle the letter of the answer to each question below the box.

MEMO

To: Employees of Peyton Discount Stores

From: Samantha Peyton, Owner of Peyton Discount Stores

Date: January 30

Subject: Shoplifting Reminders

There was a shoplifting attempt in the hardware department of our Louisville store last month. This is a good opportunity to remind you about our company's procedures. We have established guidelines for handling a suspected shoplifter in our stores.

In a situation in which a suspected shoplifter is still present in the store, follow these guidelines: Make every effort to delay his or her departure from the store. This will allow time for the proper authorities to arrive at the scene. However, at no time should your safety be at risk. Do not confront, accuse, or physically prevent the suspect from leaving the scene.

If a shoplifter leaves the store, follow these guidelines: Remain inside the store. If you are able to see the suspect's vehicle, take note of its make, model, and license-plate number. Attempt to assess the physical appearance of the suspect. This includes, but is not limited to, height, weight, hair color, and any other distinguishing physical features. Also note details about the suspect's clothing. Report this information to your store manager.

Your cooperation with these procedures is greatly appreciated.

---

1. What is the main purpose of business memos?

  A to entertain

  B to persuade

  C to explain

  D to describe

2. The author's intention for writing this memo is to

  F instill fear in employees when confronting shoplifters.

  G force employees to follow a company policy.

  H make sure managers are ready to reward brave employees.

  J remind employees to follow a company policy.

Write for Work

Your manager has asked you to write a memo or an e-mail about an upcoming company picnic. The picnic will be held on the grounds of Playland State Park. Think about what details you need to include in the memo. What do your fellow employees need to know? Think about your purpose for writing and about what should be included in a well-written memo. Write the memo in a notebook.

  Reading Extension

Turn to "Escape to Freedom" on page 73 of *Reading Basics Intermediate 1 Reader*. After you have read and/or listened to the article, answer the questions below.

Circle the letter of the answer to each question.

1. What do you think the author's intention was for writing this article?

   A to describe Douglass's achievements as a free man

   B to convince readers that slavery is wrong

   C to describe the rough conditions of slavery

   D to tell how Douglass became free

2. What is the effect of the language in paragraph 14?

   F a feeling of anger

   G a feeling of suspense

   H a feeling of sadness

   J a feeling of happiness

3. What is the purpose of paragraphs 5 and 6?

   A to entertain readers with details of Douglass's trip

   B to persuade readers that "free papers" are important

   C to explain how Douglass planned to get papers and escape

   D to describe what it was like to be an American sailor

Write the answer to each question.

4. What effect might the author's use of the quotation at the end of the article have on readers?

   _____

5. What do you think the author's purpose was for including the story about the German blacksmith who saw Douglass?

   _____

Explore Words

LONG e AND LONG i SPELLED -y

The letter *y* can stand for the long *e* or the long *i* sound, usually at the end of a word or syllable. For example, the letter *y* stands for the long -sound in *happy* and the long *i* sound in *cry*.

Read the words. If the letter *y* stands for the long -e sound, write *long e*. If it stands for the long -i sound, write *long i*.

1. reply _____

2. county _____

3. fifty _____

4. myself _____

5. gladly _____

6. why _____

SUFFIXES -ful, -ness

A suffix is a word part that can be added to the end of many words. Suffixes change the meanings of words to which they are added. For example, the suffix *-ful* means "full of," so *joyful* means "full of joy." The suffix *-ness* means "the state of being," so *sadness* means "the state of being sad."

Write a new word by adding the suffix *-ful* or *-ness* to each word.

1. care _____

2. fond _____

3. sick _____

4. help _____

5. thought _____

6. ill _____

CONTEXT CLUES

You may come across unfamiliar words as you read. You can use other words in the same sentence or in a nearby sentence to figure out what these words mean.

Read the passage. Then write the meaning of each underlined word on the line.

All green plants <u>manufacture</u> their own food. They make food by <u>combining</u>, or joining, soil nutrients, water, carbon dioxide, and sunlight. Some other plants are <u>incapable</u> of using sunlight to make food, so they live off other plants that can. They help dead plants to <u>decompose</u>. That decay is an important stage in nature's life cycle.

1. The word <u>manufacture</u> means _____.

2. The word <u>combining</u> means _____.

3. The word <u>incapable</u> means _____.

4. The word <u>decompose</u> means _____.

SPELLING: WORD ENDINGS

You can add *-ed* or *-ing* to most verbs to change the tense. You can add *-er* or *-est* to most short adjectives to compare two or more things. Sometimes you have to change the spelling of a base word when you add these endings. Read these spelling rules:

- When a word ends with silent *e*, drop the *e*. Then add the ending. For example, *slide / sliding* and *fine / finest*.

- When a word ends in a consonant followed by *y*, change the *y* to *i*. Then add the ending. The rule does NOT apply when you add the ending *-ing*. For example, *cry / cried / crying*.

- To add an ending to a word that ends with a consonant that comes after one vowel, double the consonant. For example, *shop / shopper* and *blog / blogging*.

Add the ending to each word. Write the new word on the line.

1. great + ness _____

2. freeze + ing _____

3. thick + est _____

4. cloudy + ness _____

5. copy + ed _____

6. annoy + ing _____

7. thank + ful _____

8. early + est _____

9. mad + er _____

10. brag + ed _____

ACADEMIC VOCABULARY

Knowing these high-frequency words will help you in many school subjects.

convey to make an idea or feeling known to someone

intention a goal or plan

purpose the reason something is done

describe to tell about something including its characteristics

persuade to convince someone to do something through reasoning

Complete the sentences below using one of the words above.

1. Jani had no _____ of returning the book until she was finished reading it.

2. The _____ of the trip was to meet with clients and drive new business.

3. The candidate did his best to _____ voters to vote for him.

4. Please _____ my gratitude to Tuan for making the party.

5. There was no picture, so I had to _____ the house to my brother.

Lesson 2.6

Read Graphs

Graphs show information visually. There are different kinds of graphs, including bar graphs, line graphs, and circle graphs. A bar graph organizes information along a vertical axis, which runs up and down one side, and a horizontal axis, which usually runs along the bottom. Information is shown on a set of bars. (The graphs on this page are bar graphs.) A line graph also has a vertical axis and a horizontal axis. The changing data is shown on a continuous line. (The graph on page 120 is a line graph.) A circle graph is divided into pieces, like a pie. Each piece represents a different part of the whole. When the parts of a circle graph are expressed in percentages, the parts add up to 100 percent. (The graph on page 119 is a circle graph.)

You will encounter graphs as you read. The graph might stand alone, or it might illustrate information in an article. When you read a graph you should examine the axes. Each graph has its own scale. The labels on the axes show you what the scale is.

In the graph on the left, the title indicates what the graph shows: how many dogs were at the dog park. The labels along the bottom of the graph show which days of the week are being evaluated. Each line on the vertical axis represents five dogs. To find how many dogs a bar represents, find the top of the line and trace over to the left with your finger. If a bar falls between two lines, you may need to estimate the value.

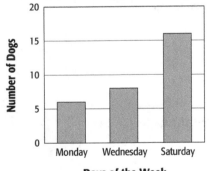

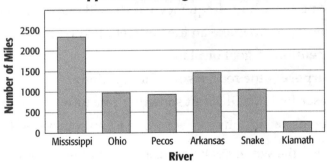

Examine the graph on the right. How many miles does each line on the vertical axis represent? Which river on the graph is the shortest? Which is the longest?

Each line represents 500 miles. Notice that each number label is 500 more than the number below it. The Klamath River is the shortest. The bar representing its length is much shorter than the other bars. The Mississippi River is the longest. Its bar is the longest on the graph.

Examine the circle graph. Then answer the questions.

Jackson Family Budget

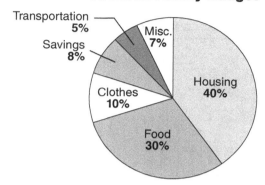

1. What does the graph show?

   _____

2. What do the sections represent?

   _____

3. What percent of their budget does the Jackson family put toward savings?

   _____

4. On which category does the family spend the most money?

   _____

5. On which category does the family spend the least money?

   _____

6. On which category does the family spend exactly 7% of their expenses?

   _____

7. On which category does the family spend exactly twice as much as they do on transportation?

   _____

8. What percentage of the family's expenses is spent on both food and housing combined?

   _____

A line graph shows changes over time.

Examine the line graph. Then answer the questions that follow.

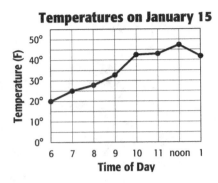

Temperatures on January 15

1. What does the graph show?

_____

2. What does the horizontal axis show?

_____

3. What does the vertical axis show?

_____

4. About what temperature was it at 7 A.M.?

_____

5. At what time of day was the highest temperature reached?

_____

6. Between which two hours did the temperature increase the most?

_____

7. What was the approximate difference in temperature between noon and 6 A.M.?

_____

8. At what time was the temperature about 33°F?

_____

The graph shows the number of people signed up for fitness activities at the city recreation center. Examine the graph. Then circle the letter of the answer to each question.

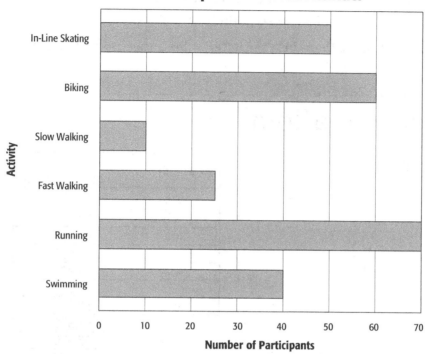

Participation-in-Fitness Activities

1. What type of graph is this?

   A line graph

   B circle graph

   C bar graph

   D pictograph

2. According to the graph, which activity has the most participants?

   F biking

   G swimming

   H fast walking

   J running

3. How many people are signed up for fast walking?

   A 60

   B 30

   C 25

   D 20

4. How many more people are signed up for running than for slow walking?

   F 45

   G 60

   H 80

   J 95

5. Which activity has exactly four times the number of participants as slow walking?

   A swimming

   B fast walking

   C running

   D biking

6. Which activity has 50 participants?

   F in-line skating

   G biking

   H running

   J swimming

Workplace Skill: Use a Sales Graph

Companies use graphs to show, compare, and contrast information. A line graph uses points connected by a line to show how a value changes over time. Some graphs include a table that lists the exact values of each point to help you.

Read the line graph about milk sales. Then circle the letter of the answer to each question below the box.

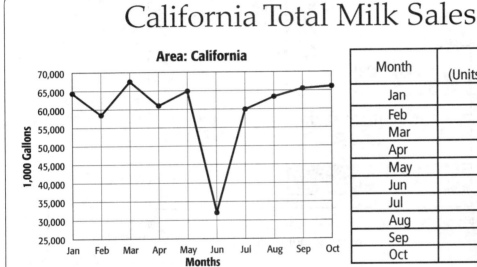

California Total Milk Sales

Area: California

Month	Sales (Units: 1,000 Gal.)
Jan	64,393
Feb	58,478
Mar	67,504
Apr	60,991
May	64,885
Jun	32,001
Jul	59,947
Aug	63,356
Sep	65,539
Oct	66,108

1. What does this graph show?

A total California milk sales by month for most of one year

B California milk sales during the summer months

C how milk sales differ for individual California cities

D California milk sales for November and December

2. What change occurred in California milk sales from the beginning of May to the beginning of June?

F milk sales increased sharply

G milk sales in June were the same as February

H milk sales went down sharply

J milk sales remained even from May to July

Write the answer to the question.

3. What reason might the creator of the graph have had for including the table of gallons sold?

_____

Write for Work

Your company is giving a presentation to employees on past trends in the California milk industry. To prepare for this, they have asked you to present information on milk sales. Use the graph on page 122 to analyze what was happening in milk sales in California. Write this information in a notebook.

Workplace Extension

The Presentation

Shelia O'Connell works for a local food and agricultural agency. She was asked to give a presentation on trends in the California milk industry. She was nervous. She had never presented information to a large group before. She did not have a great deal of time to prepare and practice. The conference was just a week away. She decided to make a plan. First she would take time to analyze the current trends in the industry. Then she would organize her information in a slideshow presentation. Finally, she would do a practice presentation for a friend and ask for critical feedback on her performance.

Circle the letter of the answer to each question.

1. How would you consider Shelia's overall preparation for the presentation?

   A   Her plan was poorly organized and thoughtless.

   B   Her plan was well organized and planned.

   C   Her plan did not take time to analyze the trends.

   D   She did not organize her information in a productive way.

2. Was it important for Shelia to practice her presentation before a friend?

   F   Yes; she and her friend could have a lot of fun and laughs that way.

   G   No; it would not help her to make a better presentation.

   H   No; she felt comfortable speaking to large groups.

   J   Yes; she could get critical feedback on her performance.

Write the answer to the question.

3. What might happen if Shelia does not practice her slideshow presentation?

   _____

   _____

   _____

Explore Words

CONSONANT PAIRS sc, mb

Some consonant pairs include a silent letter. For example, sometimes the *c* is silent in the consonant pair *sc*, as in *scenery*. The *b* is silent in the consonant pair *mb*, as in *lamb*.

Write a word from the box next to its definition. Then circle the silent consonant in your answer.

scent	limb	science	numb	scene	comb

1. a portion of a play _____

2. having no feeling _____

3. a tool for fixing hair _____

4. an arm or a leg _____

5. an odor _____

6. a school subject _____

BASE WORDS

A base word is a word that has no prefixes, suffixes, or other word endings. A base word is a word that can stand alone and have meaning. For example, the base word in *sadness* is *sad*. The base word in *rearrange* is *arrange*. The base word in *driving* is *drive*.

Read each word. Then circle the base word.

1. subway

2. laughed

3. cheerful

4. precook

5. fastest

6. replayed

7. stronger

8. worrying

9. kindness

10. speeding

11. retry

12. eating

SPELLING: PLURALS

Plural means "more than one." You can form the plural of most words by adding *-s* to them, for example, *jacket / jackets*. Add *-es* to words that end in *s*, *ss*, *sh*, *x*, or *ch*, for example, *class / classes*. To form the plural of words that end in *y*, change the *y* to *i* and add *-es*, for example, *party / parties*.

Write the plural form of each word.

1. painter _____

2. butterfly _____

3. address _____

4. berry _____

5. watch _____

6. story _____

SPELLING: CONTRACTIONS

A contraction is a shorter way to write two words. Every contraction includes an apostrophe ('). The apostrophe takes the place of letters that are dropped when you form the contraction. For example, the contraction *I'm* stands for the words *I am*. The apostrophe takes the place of the letter *a* in the word *am*.

Write a contraction from the box for each pair of words below.

couldn't	haven't	shouldn't	they'll	I've
hasn't	didn't	you're	we'll	they're

1. should not _____
2. did not _____
3. we will _____
4. has not _____
5. they are _____

6. you are _____
7. could not _____
8. have not _____
9. I have _____
10. they will _____

ACADEMIC VOCABULARY

Knowing these high-frequency words will help you in many school subjects.

graph   a visual way to show data

data   facts and statistics collected together

illustrate   to explain or make clear

label   word or words that indicate what things represent

estimate   to roughly calculate the value of something

Complete the sentences below using one of the words above.

1. Jamal used slides to _____ the information he gave in his presentation.

2. The researcher analyzed the _____ she collected in her study.

3. Eun Hee wrote a _____ on the map to show the city where she lived.

4. Karen made a _____ to show company sales for the last two months.

5. The restaurant manager had to _____ how many glasses he would need to order.

Unit 2 Review

Identify Sequence

The order in which events take place is called sequence. When you read, it is important to understand what happens first, second, third, and so on. Look for clue words such as *first, next, then,* and *last.* You also need to understand sequence to correctly follow directions.

Use Supporting Evidence

When a writer expresses an opinion or makes a statement in writing, he or she must support it with evidence. As a reader, you need to think carefully about what the writer is trying to say. Then decide if the evidence presented is logical and strong enough to support his or her position. Think carefully about whether evidence supports, denies, or is neutral to the point the writer is trying to make.

Identify Style Techniques

Writers use words, types of sentences, and punctuation to create a certain feeling in their writing. Individual writers choose the style techniques that best communicate their ideas. Writing styles can be formal or informal. The style may depend on the type of writing, the writer's purpose, and the writer's own preferences. Writers may use more than one style technique when they write.

Make Generalizations

A generalization is a statement that applies to many people, events, or situations. To make a generalization, you put together a number of facts or examples to reach a logical conclusion. Look for these signal words: *most, many, few, all, usually,* and *generally.*

Recognize Author's Purpose, Effect, and Intention

Authors typically write for one or more of the following purposes: to persuade, to inform, to explain, to entertain, or to describe. Authors reveal their intentions by using style techniques to create a particular effect in their writing.

Read Graphs

Graphs are a way to give information visually. There are many different kinds of graphs, including line graphs, bar graphs, and circle graphs (also called pie charts). Line graphs show change over time. Bar graphs compare different categories of data. Circle graphs show parts of a whole.

Unit 2 Assessment

Read each passage. Then circle the letter of the answer to each question.

> Arthur Ashe was a world-famous tennis player. In 1968 he became the first African American to win the U.S. Men's National singles championship. In 1975 Ashe became the first African American man to win the Wimbledon singles championship in England. Ashe was born in Richmond, Virginia, in 1943. As a college student he won both the NCAA singles and doubles championships in 1966. He retired from tennis in 1980 and was elected to the International Tennis Hall of Fame five years later. Arthur Ashe died in 1993.

1. Which of these titles did Arthur Ashe win last?

  A Wimbledon singles

  B NCAA doubles

  C NCAA singles

  D U.S. Men's National singles

2. In what year was Ashe elected to the International Tennis Hall of Fame?

  F 1943

  G 1966

  H 1975

  J 1985

> Clara Barton was a nurse and is famous for founding the American Red Cross. Barton began serious nursing work during the Civil War. She cared for badly wounded soldiers. She was known as the Angel of the Battlefield. After the war, she set up a group to search for missing soldiers. Later Barton learned about the International Red Cross. It was an international group of volunteers who helped the wounded in any war without regard to their nationality. She persuaded the U.S. government to follow the same rules. In 1881 Barton became the first president of the American Red Cross. The organization eventually began helping people in disasters other than war.

3. The author's purpose for writing this passage was

  A to persuade people that the Civil War was a terrible event.

  B to describe Clara Barton's role in founding the American Red Cross.

  C to explain how to set up an international organization.

  D to describe the life of Clara Barton.

4. Which evidence from the passage supports the fact that Clara Barton became known as the "Angel of the Battlefield"?

  F She is famous for founding the American Red Cross.

  G She learned about an international group of volunteers.

  H She cared for badly wounded soldiers during the Civil War.

  J Her organization began helping people in disasters other than war.

One of the greatest inventions of all time was the railroad. Nothing like it had ever been seen before, and "the iron road" opened up the world to vast numbers of people. Until that time, most people had been rooted to their birthplaces. Other forms of travel, such as covered wagon or stagecoach, had been slow, costly, and risky. The railroad gave many people the freedom to travel. Business people all over the world soon understood the importance of railroads. They formed large railroad companies, and they worked to attract passengers. For example, George Pullman organized a company in 1867 to build sleeping cars. Railroad companies also introduced luxurious parlor cars and elegant dining service for wealthy travelers.

5. From this passage you can generalize that

  A railroad travel was designed only for business people.

  B most people did not like to travel.

  C railroad travel was faster, cheaper, and safer than earlier forms of travel.

  D railroads grew slowly throughout the world.

6. Which evidence from the passage supports the fact that customers were important to the railroad?

  F Other forms of travel had been risky and slow.

  G George Pullman organized a company in 1867 to build sleeping cars.

  H The freedom to travel was there for all to enjoy.

  J One of the greatest inventions of all time was the railroad.

I'm driving home from a long day at work. The traffic is heavy. I feel the beginning of a bad headache. I turn the corner. I slam on my brakes. Two young teens are merrily in-line skating down the middle of the street. One is spinning on a single bright pink skate, like an overly excited flamingo. The other is gyrating in some kind of wild dance. They basically block the whole street with their childish tricks as I sit steaming behind the steering wheel. Meanwhile, these goofs twirl and prance about. They grin and laugh and nod and wave as if they think they are entertaining all the drivers backed up behind them.

7. The short sentences at the beginning of the passage help to show the narrator's

  A intelligence.

  B tense frame of mind.

  C relaxed feeling.

  D sense of humor.

8. Which phrase or clause best reveals the narrator's attitude toward the skaters?

  F "these goofs twirl and prance about"

  G "slam on my brakes"

  H "a long day at work"

  J "behind the steering wheel"

Study the graphs. Then circle the letter of the answer to each question.

Types of Recycled Materials

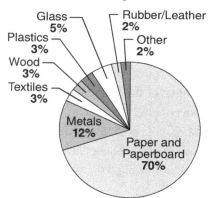

Source: U.S. Environmental Protection Agency

9. Which item on the graph makes up the largest percentage of recycled material?

 A metals

 B paper and paperboard

 C wood

 D other

10. Which items on the graph make up identical percentages of recycled material?

 F wood, glass, plastics

 G plastics, metals, other

 H rubber and leather, glass, other

 J textiles, wood, plastics

Percentage of Some Common Items Recycled (rounded to nearest 5%)

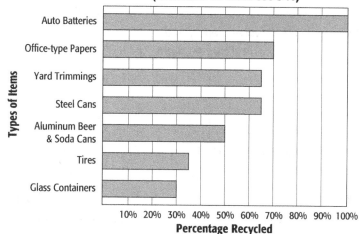

11. About what percentage of aluminum cans are recycled?

 A 25%

 B 50%

 C 90%

 D 35%

12. Which item is only about 30% recycled?

 F office-type papers

 G yard trimmings

 H glass containers

 J auto batteries

Read the e-mails. Then circle the letter of the answer to each question.

From: gina.mccloskey@metricality.com
To: andrea_phelps@writingmaster.com
Subject: WFF project

Good morning, Ms. Phelps.

I am writing to personally thank you upon the completion of the WFF project. We are delighted to say that our confidence was rewarded. Your employees are to be commended for their careful attention to detail, timely questions, and high standards. We could not be happier with the final results of the project. I can also guarantee that we will request your services again when we have the opportunity. Please share my thanks with all those who worked on the project.

Sincerely,
Gina McCloskey
Manager, Creative Services
Metricality, Inc.

From: andrea_phelps@writingmaster.com
To: WFF_Team@writingmaster.com
Subject: Job well done!

Hi, Team!

Just received a super-thrilling letter from our contact at Metricality and had to share! Basically, you all did a fantastic job on WFF, and the client is more than delighted. Pat yourselves on the back for a job well done! Believe me, I know how hard you all worked, and you deserve major kudos. Best part about it: they plan to give us more work in the future. And that's what it's all about, right?

Congrats!
Andie

---

13. What is one style technique that identifies the first e-mail as formal writing?

    A the use of slang and everyday language

    B the use of complete and complex sentences

    C the use of incomplete sentences

    D the use of punctuation for emphasis

14. The second e-mail is in an informal style because

    F The writer is writing to her coworkers.

    G The writer is looking for a new job.

    H The writer is writing to a close friend.

    J The writer is scheduling an appointment.

15. What is the writer's purpose in the second e-mail?

    A to ask the client for another project

    B to ask for more support from coworkers

    C to explain the details of the WFF project

    D to share praise with coworkers

16. What effect did the writer of the second e-mail intend to create through her informal style?

    F uneasiness

    G suspense

    H encouragement

    J discouragement

Read the excerpt from an employee handbook. Then circle the letter of the answer to each question.

> # Graceview Company Employee Handbook
>
> ## Section 1: General Information
>
> **1.9 Transportation Options**
>
> There are several good transportation options for traveling to our factory. Please see the suggestions below and consider the pros and cons of each option.
>
> **1.9a** You can take the bus. Our factory is located near the bus stop for the numbers 8 and 14 buses. Get off at Briggs Corner and walk three blocks west. You can check the bus routes and schedules online. You can also buy monthly bus passes at a discounted price.
>
> **1.9b** The Graceview Company encourages ride sharing. You can place messages for other employees on the main bulletin board. You can arrange fuel-cost sharing on your own.
>
> **1.9c** You can also drive your own car. You will find a parking garage around the corner. There is also metered street parking.
>
> **1.9d** You may wish to consider walking or biking. These options provide daily exercise. They are by far the most economical choices.
>
> Stop by Human Resources or call extension 756 for more detailed information.

17. From this memo, employees can generalize that

   A cost is the only consideration in choosing transportation.

   B everyone should walk or ride the bus to get to the factory.

   C sharing a ride is difficult to arrange.

   D there are many things to consider in choosing transportation.

18. Which sentence supports the idea that walking or biking is a good transportation option?

   F Monthly bus passes are available at a discounted price.

   G Metered street parking is also available.

   H The Graceview Company encourages ride-sharing.

   J These options provide daily exercise.

19. What is the purpose of this employee handbook excerpt?

   A to persuade employees to choose the most expensive transportation option

   B to provide employees with useful information about transportation options

   C to convince employees that ride sharing is the best choice for everyone

   D to explain how to obtain a bus schedule online

20. Which of these phrases does NOT encourage employees to think about cost?

   F "by far the most economical choices"

   G "walk three blocks west"

   H "at a discounted price"

   J "share the fuel costs"

Circle the letter of the answer to each question.

21. Which word has an *r*-controlled vowel sound?

   A prank

   B prune

   C purse

   D pry

22. Which word is a compound word?

   F owner

   G under

   H benched

   J barcode

23. Which word is an antonym of *gigantic*?

   A gentle

   B tiny

   C huge

   D automatic

24. In which word does *g* make a soft sound?

   F legal

   G garden

   H page

   J grant

25. Which word includes a silent consonant?

   A start

   B curb

   C strum

   D crumb

26. Which is the correct meaning of *prewrite*?

   F to write before

   G to write again

   H to write back

   J to write in support

27. Which form of *drip* is spelled correctly?

   A driped

   B dripped

   C driping

   D drippt

28. Which two words are homophones?

   F bounce, sauce

   G trend, send

   H prince, prints

   J bale, bill

29. Which phrase means "the notebooks that belong to the students"?

   A the student's notebooks

   B the students notebooks

   C the students' notebooks

   D the student notebooks'

30. Which is the correct meaning of *happiness*?

   F the state of being happy

   G happening now

   H being happier

   J the state of being unhappy

31. Which word is a synonym of *cautious*?

   A lazy

   B careful

   C simple

   D reckless

32. Which word contains an open first syllable?

   F bubble

   G candle

   H label

   J single

33. In which word does *y* make the long *i* sound?

   A supply

   B happy

   C carry

   D pretty

34. What is the plural form of *stash*?

   F stashs

   G stashies

   H stashes

   J stases

Unit 3

In this unit you will learn how to

You will practice the following workplace skills

You will also learn new words and their meanings and put your reading skills to work in written activities. You will get additional reading practice in *Reading Basics Intermediate 1 Reader*.

Lesson 3.1

Predict Outcomes

When you predict an outcome, you are drawing a conclusion about what the result of an event or events might be. People often predict the outcomes of movies, television programs, and sporting events. In the same way, you can predict outcomes as you read. Use clues in the text and things you know from your own life to make guesses that make sense about what will happen next in a situation.

Here are some key points to remember as you make predictions:

- Think ahead about how things might turn out. You can make predictions at any time during your reading.

- Use your prior knowledge and experience to make predictions. Think about times when you have experienced or read about a situation similar to what you are reading. Think about what happened in those situations.

- Adjust your prediction as you read. New information may be revealed that changes your prediction. Remember that predictions should make sense with regard to what you have read to that point, but they may not always turn out to be correct.

A character in a story will usually continue to act in a consistent way. For example, if a character named Tom is usually curious, you can predict what he will do when he sees an odd-shaped box sitting on the table. Most likely, he will look inside.

Use clues from the story and what you already know to predict what might happen next.

> Anita is very shy. While others chat and laugh at the bus stop, she just waits quietly. Anita has a crush on Tyee, but friends always surround him. Then one day she gets to the bus stop early, and she and Tyee are the only two people there.

Ask yourself, "What do I know from the story?" The story tells you that Anita has a crush on Tyee but that she is shy.

Ask yourself, "What do I know from previous experience?" Your experience tells you that shy people often have trouble talking to others, especially if the shy person has a crush.

You can predict that Anita will wait quietly, just as before, and hope that Tyee will speak to her.

Read each passage. Use clues from each passage and what you already know to predict what is likely to happen next. Then circle the letter of the statement that best predicts the outcome.

> Cruz daydreams often and finds it hard to pay attention in meetings. As he listens to his boss detail plans for the upcoming quarter, Cruz daydreams about being an air force pilot. He draws pictures of planes on his meeting agenda. At the end of the meeting, he has taken no notes and does not fully understand the plans. He doesn't remember much about the meeting.

1. A Cruz will quit his job and become a pilot.

   B Cruz's boss will admire his airplane doodles.

   C Cruz will convince his boss that the company needs an airplane.

   D Cruz will fall behind at work because he does not always pay attention.

> Jia Li likes to keep busy, and she enjoys being around people. She has been taking a Pilates class at the local community center and volunteering at an after-school program. Her Pilates class is ending, and the after-school program is closing down for summer vacation. This morning, she received a catalog in the mail from the local adult-education center that offers some classes she is interested in.

2. F Jia Li will sign up for an adult-education class.

   G Jia Li will complain that there is nothing to do.

   H Jia Li will start watching more television.

   J Jia Li will do exercises at home.

> Atsu loves making people laugh and being the center of attention. Today he saw a flyer for auditions at a local theater. The play is a musical comedy, and there are many types of roles. Some roles require singing. Other roles require acting but do not require singing.

3. A Atsu will attend the musical and enjoy it.

   B Atsu will audition for the musical and hope to get a role.

   C Atsu will make fun of the people who audition for the musical.

   D Atsu will discover that he does not like musicals.

Read each passage. Then circle the letter of the statement that tells what probably will happen next. Write a sentence on each line telling why you think this will happen.

Thanh likes high adventure and thrills. He has gone backpacking in the mountains, zip-lining in the jungle, and white-water kayaking. He is always the first to try new roller coasters, and he loves extreme sports. Thanh received a large bonus at work this year, and he decided to spend it on a vacation.

1. **A** Thanh will take a trip to Hollywood so he can see movies being filmed.
   B Thanh will take a trip to New York City so he can visit the Statue of Liberty.
   C Thanh will take a trip to Brazil so he can canoe down the Amazon.
   D Thanh will take a trip to Paris so he can go shopping.

_____

Efia and her roommate Naima often borrow each other's clothes. Efia is going out shortly and wants to borrow Naima's red sweater. Naima has to work late, and there is no way to reach her. Naima has never said no to Efia before, though.

2. **F** Naima will get angry with Efia for wearing her clothes.
   G Efia will buy a sweater that looks like the one she wants to borrow.
   H Efia will borrow the sweater without asking Naima.
   J Efia will get angry with Naima for getting home so late.

_____

Jazmin takes a kickboxing class at her gym every day after work. The class is very active, with a lot of aerobic activity. Today the air-conditioning in the gym is broken, and the air is humid. Jazmin is especially tired, hot, and thirsty, and she goes home right after class.

3. **A** Jazmin will check her e-mail and video chat with a friend as soon as she gets home.
   B Jazmin will drinks lots of water and take a cool shower right away.
   C Jazmin will have a big dinner as soon as she gets home.
   D Jazmin will clean the house because she is so energized from her workout.

_____

Reading Basics · Intermediate 1

Read each passage. Then circle the letter of the statement that tells the most likely outcome of the passage.

Martina buys a new dress to wear on a date. On the way home she drops the bag, and the dress falls out into a mud puddle. She washes the dress without reading the fabric care label that says *Dry Clean Only*.

1. A Martina will look chic in her new dress.

B The dirt will not come out of the dress.

C The new dress will shrink and be ruined.

D Martina will feel pleased with her solution to the problem.

Sheng and his friend Lisa have a dog-walking business. Today Sheng is supposed to take the Jones family's three dogs out at 2:00 P.M., but his car breaks down on the way. He knows he will be very late, and he knows the dogs must be taken for a walk. He uses his cell phone to make a call.

2. F Sheng will get his car towed to a mechanic and wait while the repairs are done. He will walk the dogs afterward if he has time.

G Sheng will call Lisa and find out about her schedule. He will ask her whether she will walk the dogs today.

H Sheng will call Mr. Jones. Mr. Jones will decide which member of his family will leave work early to walk the dogs.

J Sheng will receive a bonus from the Jones family at the end of the week. They will reward him for his quick thinking.

Hector invites a coworker to come to his house for dinner. He decides he will cook an elaborate meal to impress her. He chooses recipes he has never made before. When he reads through the recipes, he discovers that he does not understand all the directions. He does not take the time to look things up but guesses what to do instead. His dinner tastes very odd.

3. A The dinner will be perfect, and Hector's coworker will be impressed.

B Hector will pretend he isn't home when his coworker knocks on the door.

C Hector will discover a hidden talent for cooking.

D Hector's dinner will not be very good, and his coworker will not be impressed.

Workplace Skill: Use a Diagram to Predict Outcomes

It is often necessary to use diagrams in the workplace. Diagrams can be plans, drawings, sketches, or outlines to show how things work. Diagrams can tell you how to use something, like office equipment, or how to fix something that is not operating properly. You can combine clues in the diagram with what you already know to make a prediction—a guess about what might happen next. Use the picture and words in the diagram to think ahead about possible outcomes for your actions.

Read the diagram. Then circle the letter of the answer to each question.

Printer Misfeed Diagram

(12) Paper misfeed in tray 1

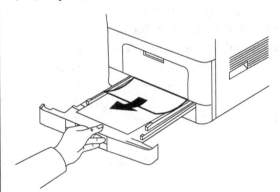

Pull tray 1 gently until it stops.
Remove the misfed paper.

✓ Be sure to check the following warning(s) before proceeding.

Before removing the misfed paper in tray 1: Check for a paper misfeed in the transport area. If you pull the tray out without checking, you may tear misfed paper and make it more difficult to remove the pieces that remain in the machine.
See (11) Paper misfeed in the transport area.

1. Adam is rushing to print copies of a report for a meeting, and the printer misfeeds. He pulls out the tray and starts to remove the misfeed. What might happen next?

   A A green light will go on.

   B He might tear the paper.

   C The printer will shut down.

   D The printer will restart.

2. What is important to do before removing the misfed paper in tray 1?

   F Check the transport area.

   G Pull tray 1 gently.

   H Pull trays 1 and 2 gently.

   J Open a new ream of copy paper.

Write for Work

Review the diagram on page 138. In a notebook, write a summary of what the diagram shows. Include all the important steps.

 Reading Extension

Turn to "A Horrible Way to Die" on page 81 of *Reading Basics Intermediate 1 Reader*. After you have read and/or listened to the article, answer the questions below.

Circle the letter of the answer to each question.

1. Based on the article, what do you predict will happen if people continue to cut down the rain forests?

    A People will become immune to Ebola.

    B People will be exposed to new diseases.

    C Many diseases will be wiped out.

    D Nothing will happen.

2. What did the doctors predict would happen if people continued to bury their dead in the traditional way?

    F Contact with blood from the bodies would spread the disease.

    G The people would develop an immunity to the virus.

    H The virus would seep into the dirt and infect crops.

    J The virus would get into the water supply when people washed their hands.

3. Why did doctors urge people to wear rubber gloves to bury their dead?

    A to increase the sale of rubber gloves

    B to keep the dead bodies clean

    C to prevent their skin from touching the infected bodies

    D to prevent them from damaging the dead bodies

Write the answer to each question.

4. Reread paragraph 10. What did you predict would happen?

    _____

    _____

5. Reread paragraphs 12 and 13. What did you predict would happen with the disease?

    _____

    _____

Explore Words

VOWEL COMBINATIONS

In words that end in silent *e*, such as *lake*, the vowel stands for a long vowel sound. Vowel combinations can also stand for a long vowel sound. For example, the vowel pair *ai* stands for the long *a* sound in *rainbow*. The vowel combinations below usually stand for long vowel sounds. Notice that the vowel *o* combines with the consonant *w* to stand for the long *o* sound:

long *a*: *ai, ay*   **long *o*:** *oa, oe, ow*   **long *i*:** *ie*   **long *e*:** *ea, ee, ie*   **long *u*:** *ue*

Circle the word in each sentence that has the same vowel sound as the underlined word.

1. Marcos <u>leased</u> a blue car this weekend.
2. He was clueless about the <u>rule</u>.
3. My <u>goal</u> is to throw a curve ball.
4. Monique eats whole <u>grains</u> every day.
5. We tried to fix the toaster <u>twice</u>.
6. You need to give a <u>brief</u> answer.

SYLLABLES

When a two-syllable word has two vowels separated by two consonants, divide the word between the two consonants: in/side. The first syllable is closed and has a short vowel sound. When one consonant separates the vowels in a word, try dividing it before and after the consonant to see which sounds right. For example, should *wagon* be wa/gon or wag/on? The answer is wag/on. For the word *profile*, the answer is be different. The first syllable in pro/file is open and has a long vowel sound.

Draw a slash mark to divide the word into syllables. Then circle *short* or *long* to describe the vowel sound in the first syllable. The first item has been done for you.

1. pi/lot   short   (long)
2. indent   short   long
3. token   short   long
4. donate   short   long

CONTEXT CLUES

If a sentence includes a word you do not know, look for context clues. Context clues are other words in the sentence or surrounding sentences that help you figure out the meaning of the unknown word. Look at this sentence: *Kia's rude comments surprised me since she is always so civil.* Context clues help you guess that *civil* means "polite."

Use context clues to find the meaning of each underlined word. Circle the correct meaning.

1. Wrap the <u>fragile</u> gift in several layers of paper to protect it. (huge, delicate)
2. He was <u>ravenous</u>, so he ate two sandwiches. (tired, hungry)
3. Even when you want to give up, you must <u>persevere</u>. (continue, stop)

SYNONYMS AND ANTONYMS

Synonyms are words that have the same or almost the same meanings. For example, *start* and *begin* are synonyms. Antonyms are words that have opposite or nearly opposite meanings. For example, *start* and *stop* are antonyms.

Choose one word from the box that is a synonym and another word that is an antonym for each numbered word. Write the words on the lines.

silent	hot	accept	full	chilly
noisy	destroy	vacant	refuse	construct

	Synonym	**Antonym**
1. build	_____	_____
2. cold	_____	_____
3. reject	_____	_____
4. quiet	_____	_____
5. empty	_____	_____

ACADEMIC VOCABULARY

Knowing these high-frequency words will help you in many school subjects.

predict   to make a guess about something that will happen based on clues or experience

outcome   result

prior   previous

adjust   to alter slightly

reveal   to make information known to others

Complete the sentences below using one of the words above.

1. The _____ of the match determined which player advanced to the next round.

2. After her brother used her car, Johanna needed to _____ the rearview mirror.

3. Weather forecasters _____ the weather, but they aren't always right.

4. Before the class, Rafael had no _____ experience welding.

5. The magician would not _____ how he did his illusions.

Lesson 3.2

Identify Cause and Effect

INTRODUCE

Understanding cause and effect means understanding how events relate to one another. When you read, you identify cause and effect by finding out why, when, or how something happened. Writers often use signal words to show cause-and-effect relationships. These are some examples: *as a result, due to, so, because, if, then, therefore, consequently, since,* and *thus.* You can use these words and phrases to help you identify causes and effects in your reading. There may be cause-and-effect relationships not called out by these signal words.

Sometimes an effect has a direct and obvious cause. If you trip over something and fall down, you know the cause of your fall and feel the effect. Sometimes a cause and an effect may be harder to identify. Ask yourself these questions: *What has happened? What is the cause? What is the effect? Is there a direct relationship between them?* Note that a cause may have more than one effect.

Cause	Effects
The world population doubles in size.	Countries are overcrowded. Food is in short supply. Diseases spread easily.

An effect may result from several causes.

Causes	Effect
Asian elephants are hunted for their tusks. They reproduce slowly. Their habitats are destroyed.	Asian elephants are in danger of becoming extinct.

Read the passage. Then circle the signal words the writer uses to show cause and effect.

> This morning I was late for work because there was an electrical problem on the subway, and the subway train stopped. As a result, I was stuck on the train for almost an hour. Finally, the train started again, and I was able to get off at my stop. Because I was in such a hurry, I tripped on the curb. Consequently, all my papers went flying, and I had to run around gathering them up.

Did you circle *because, as a result,* and *consequently*? The author uses these words to explain the multiple effects of the electrical problem on the subway.

Study each set of events. Then list the causes and the effects.

1. The days grew shorter, and the weather turned colder. The geese flew south.

Causes: _____

_____

Effect: _____

2. The furnace stopped working. The pipes in the house froze, and the houseplants died.

Cause: _____

Effects: _____

_____

3. Heavy rain flooded the town. Houses were destroyed, and drinking water was scarce. People were evacuated.

Cause: _____

Effects: _____

_____

_____

4. When the orphaned ducks hatched, I was the first thing they saw. The ducklings followed me everywhere because they thought I was their mother.

Cause: _____

Effects: _____

_____

5. A big discount store opened outside the town. As a result, several small shops downtown lost business and failed. Now people have to shop at the discount store, which is impersonal and less convenient.

Cause: _____

Effects: _____

_____

_____

Read the passage. Then fill in the missing causes and effects in the graphic organizer. Causes should be on the left side of the chart and effects on the right side.

Why does Earth have living things? One reason is its distance from the sun, which is 146 million kilometers (96 million miles) away. This distance is ideal because it allows Earth's surface to have a life-friendly range of temperatures. On average, the temperature on Earth is about 13°C to 17°C (55°F to 62°F). Water can exist in a liquid state at these temperatures. All living things depend on liquid water.

Another reason life thrives on Earth is the oxygen-rich atmosphere. Most living things, even those in the water, need oxygen to survive. In addition, a form of oxygen called ozone helps protect Earth from the sun's harmful ultraviolet (UV) rays. Ozone collects in an upper layer of the atmosphere.

The moon also affects living things. It helps keep Earth's axis pointing in the same direction as it moves through its orbit. Without the pull of the moon's gravity, Earth's axis might wobble back and forth from day to day. Living things might not be able to adapt to the severe changes in weather and climate this would cause.

Causes	Effects
1. _____ _____	Earth's surface has a life-friendly range of temperatures.
The average temperature is 13°C to 17°C (55°F to 62°F).	2. _____ _____
Earth has an oxygen-rich atmosphere.	3. _____ _____
Ozone collects in the upper layer of the atmosphere.	4. _____ _____
5. _____ _____	Earth's axis points in the same direction as it moves through its orbit.

Read all four sentences in each item. Which one is the cause or effect of all the other events? Circle the letter of the answer to each question.

1. Which of the following is the cause of all the other events?

   A I was late for work.

   B I missed the train.

   C I overslept this morning.

   D I had to skip breakfast.

2. Which of the following is the effect of all the other events?

   F Traffic was heavy and it made me very angry.

   G Sunlight was glaring off the windshields.

   H I had a terrible headache by the time I reached work.

   J Exhaust fumes filled the air.

3. Which of the following is the cause of all the other events?

   A I was determined to buy the red truck.

   B I saved half my paycheck every week.

   C I asked for cash for my birthday.

   D I quit spending money on junk food, games, and CDs.

4. Which of the following is the effect of all the other events?

   F The puppy was finally housebroken.

   G I took the puppy out every hour.

   H I praised the puppy every time it went outside.

   J I scolded the puppy when it had accidents in the house.

5. Which of the following is the cause of all the other events?

   A I checked interesting cookbooks out of the library.

   B I watched Mama closely when she cooked my favorite dishes.

   C I began making simple meals.

   D I decided it was time to learn to cook.

6. Which of the following is the effect of all the other events?

   F Asian beetles attacked the tree.

   G Woodpeckers pecked many holes in the tree.

   H Lightning struck the tree.

   J The weakened tree died.

Workplace Skill: Identify Cause and Effect in a Policy

A policy is a documented set of guidelines formulated by a company. When you read policies and procedures, look for causes and effects. Try to identify the reasons for the rules and what effects they have on business practices and on you as an employee.

Read the attendance policy. Use context clues to figure out the meaning of unfamiliar words. Then circle the letter of the answer to each question below the box.

Attendance Policy

A Chip Off the Block Bakery

Policy and Procedures Manual

A Chip Off the Block Bakery expects every employee to be regular and punctual in attendance. We expect you to be on time for your shift. This means being in the bakery and ready to work at your starting time each day. That way we can continue to provide our customers with the top-notch service they've come to expect. Absenteeism and tardiness place a burden on other employees as well as on the company.

Employees are expected to work their regularly scheduled shifts unless other arrangements have been made with a supervisor. If you know you will be unable to work your shift, please give at least 24 hours notice. This allows us to find another employee to fill your shift.

We recognize that employees may be late or absent due to illness or the illness of a dependent family member. In the event of one of these situations, please call a supervisor as soon as you know you will not be available. You are responsible for speaking directly with your supervisor. If your supervisor cannot be reached, you should leave a voice mail or an e-mail message notifying him or her of your absence/tardiness.

---

1. What is the cause of wanting employees to be on time for their shift?

   A   Supervisors need to know if they need to fill a shift.

   B   Employees should work their regularly scheduled shift.

   C   The bakery needs to provide good customer service.

   D   Other employees will sometimes be absent due to personal illness.

2. As used in the policy, what is the meaning of the word *punctual*?

   F   neatly dressed

   G   on time

   H   regularly late

   J   good at baking

Write for Work

You are a supervisor at A Chip Off the Block Bakery. Recently some employees have been forgetting to call in their absences or give 24-hour notice. In a notebook, write a memo or e-mail to all your employees reminding them about the attendance policy and procedures. Make sure the employees understand the importance of good attendance in the workplace.

  # Reading Extension

Turn to "A Shocking Experience" on page 89 of *Reading Basics Intermediate 1 Reader*. After you have read and/or listened to the article, answer the questions below.

Circle the letter of the answer to each question.

1. Which was NOT an effect of lightning strikes on Roy Sullivan?

    A His hair and eyebrows were singed.

    B He lost a big toe.

    C His shoulder was burned.

    D He lost his sight.

2. What was one effect Sherri Spain experienced after being hit by lightning?

    F She regained her sight.

    G Her clothes caught on fire.

    H Her hair turned blond.

    J Her hearing improved.

3. What caused Edwin Robinson to lose his sight?

    A He was born blind.

    B He was in a car crash.

    C He was hit by lightning.

    D He had meningitis.

Write the answer to each question.

4. What causes Florida to have more storms than any other state?

_____

5. What is one effect that being hit by lightning had on Edwin Robinson?

_____

Explore Words

VOWEL COMBINATIONS

The vowel combination *ow* often stands for the long *o* sound. However, vowel combinations *ow* and *ou* sometimes stand for different sounds—the sounds you hear at the end of *cow* and in the middle of *house*. Vowel combinations *oy* and *oi* stand for different sounds—the sounds you hear at the end of *boy* and in the middle of *noise*.

Choose a vowel combination to complete each word. Write it on the line.

1. You look angry when you fr_____n. (ow, oy)

2. The cat weighs eight p_____nds. (ou, oi)

3. I am enj_____ing my computer class. (ow, oy)

4. What is the p_____nt of that game? (ou, oi)

SILENT LETTERS

The consonant pairs *wr*, *gn*, and *kn* in words such as *write*, *gnat*, and *knee* each stand for one sound. Notice that the first letter in each pair is silent. The letters *tch* and *dge* each stand for one sound and have a silent letter (the *t* in *tch* and the *d* in *dge*). These letters appear at the end of syllables and in one-syllable words such as *badge* and *pitch*.

Complete each sentence with the word that has a silent consonant. Circle the word and underline the silent consonant.

1. We rode our bikes across the (road, bridge).

2. Luis fell off his bike and sprained his (wrist, hand).

3. Sailors know different ways to tie (ropes, knots).

4. An annoying (fly, gnat) buzzed and buzzed around the kitchen.

5. Remember to (fix, patch) your torn jeans.

6. Did Rosa (sign, mail) the application form?

SPELLING: HOMOPHONES

Homophones are words that sound alike but have different meanings and spellings. For example, *one* and *won* are homophones. The word *one* is a number, while *won* is the past tense form of *win*.

Read each group of words. Circle the two homophones.

1. knight   kite   note   night

2. buy   baby   boy   by

3. chili   hilly   chilly   hill

4. plain   pain   plane   airplane

5. nose   nice   knows   noise

A prefix is a word part added to the beginning of a word. Prefixes change the meanings of the words. The prefix *post-* means "after," *re-* means "again" or "back," and *un-* means "not."

Add a prefix to each word in the right-hand column to make it match the meaning of the phrase. Write the new word on the line.

1. play again   _____   play

2. not happy   _____   happy

3. think again   _____   think

4. after the war   _____   war

5. pay back   _____   pay

6. not known   _____   known

7. not fair   _____   fair

8. after the game   _____   game

9. write again   _____   write

ACADEMIC VOCABULARY

Knowing these high-frequency words will help you in many school subjects.

cause   a person, thing, or event that produces an effect

effect   a result or consequence

relate   to be connected

obvious   easily seen, recognized, or understood

determine   to work out or establish exactly

Complete the sentences below using one of the words above.

1. The _____ of the accident was unclear.

2. Beno felt silly when he realized there was a(n) _____ solution he had missed.

3. The doctor tried to _____ the cause of the outbreak.

4. The _____ of too much sun is a bad burn.

5. The author of the article tried hard to _____ the two subjects to one another.

Lesson 3.3

Understand Consumer Materials

A consumer is a person who buys goods and services for his or her own use. All people are consumers, whether they purchase a lot or a little. People buy, or consume, things they need and want. Printed or electronic materials often come with what you buy. There are many different kinds of consumer materials, including advertisements, coupons, product labels, instructions, and owner's manuals.

It is important to read consumer materials carefully. They may contain information that you need in order to use or maintain your product or service. They may give safety tips. Many consumer materials have parts that are written in small print. The information contained in the small print is as important as—or sometimes more important than—the information in larger type.

Most packaged food you buy will have a nutrition label on it. Nutrition labels contain information about the fat, calories, and vitamins in food, as well as valuable information about the size of one serving.

Read the nutrition label for a box of cereal. Then answer the questions.

Nutrition Facts

Serving Size	1 cup (54 g/1.9 oz.)
Servings Per Container	About 9

Amount Per Serving	Cereal
Calories 190	Calories from Fat 10

Total Fat 1g	2%
Saturated Fat 0g	0%
Cholesterol 0mg	0%
Sodium 5mg	0%
Potassium 210mg	6%
Total Carbohydrate 44g	15%
Dietary Fiber 5g	24%
Sugars 9g	
Other Carbohydrate 30g	
Protein 5g	

Vitamin A (100% as Beta-carotene)	10%
Vitamin C	0%

Ingredients: Whole grain wheat, brown sugar, whole oats, sugar, honey

How many servings are in this box of cereal?

What do *g* and *oz* stand for?

What does *mg* stand for?

How much potassium is in one serving of this cereal?

What percentage of your daily potassium requirement does this cereal give you?

There are nine servings in the box. The number of servings is listed near the top of the label. The abbreviation *g* stands for *gram*; *oz* stands for *ounce*; and *mg* stands for *milligram*, one thousandth of a gram. These are units of measure. One serving of this cereal has 210 milligrams of potassium. This quantity is 6 percent of your daily requirement. The column on the right tells the percentage of your daily requirements that one serving of this food provides.

Coupons often have small print that contains restrictions on how you can use the coupon.

Read the coupon. Then answer the questions.

Dazzle

15% OFF

your full-price purchase of $100 or more.

Valid online and in-store. To redeem, present coupon to cashier. Cashier, enter code **1058365020**. To redeem online, enter code **1085739422** during checkout.

Coupon valid until November 10. Valid only at Dazzle stores or at www.dazzle.com. Coupon must be present at time of in-store purchase. Not valid on sale items. To receive 15% off, full-priced purchase must total $100 or more. Not valid for purchase of gift cards. Not valid on prior purchases. Not valid on credit card payments. Reproductions of coupons are not valid. Cannot be combined with other offers.

---

1. When should you enter the code if you want to use this coupon online?

_____

2. If you buy $80 worth of full-priced clothes and $20 worth of sale items, will you get to use the coupon? Why or why not?

_____

3. If you buy $110 worth of full-priced items and $75 worth of sale items, will you get to use the coupon? Will you get to use it on your entire purchase? Explain.

_____

4. If you bought $125 worth of full-priced items last week, can you use the coupon? Why or why not?

_____

5. What are two things you must do if you want to use this coupon?

_____

Credit card companies sometimes send letters to people. The companies want people to sign up for their credit cards.

Read the following parts of a chart printed in small type on the back of a letter from a credit card company. Then answer the questions.

Take advantage of our credit card!	
Put all your credit charges on one card. You will enjoy an APR (annual percentage rate) as low as 0%* on transferred balances for six months. Monthly payments must be made to keep this low rate. Transfer your balances from other credit cards to ours! See how much you save!	
*Annual Percentage Rate	Promotional rate of 0% for 6 months if you transfer balances of $4000 or more; 3.9% if you transfer balances of less than $4000. Rate for new purchases: 12.99%–22.99% Rate for cash advances: 19.99% If you default**, up to 23.99% for new purchases.
Variable Rate Information	The annual percentage rate for purchases may vary monthly. We calculate the rate by adding 9.74% to the U.S. Prime Rate published by the *Wall Street Journal* on the last business day of each month. That rate currently is 3.25%.

1. What are "transferred balances"?

_____

2. If you transferred a balance of $2,000 from another credit card, what rate of interest would you

pay on this balance? _____

3. What symbol found in the claim about the annual percentage rate means that details about the

claim are somewhere else in the letter? _____

4. What interest rate do you pay on new purchases made with this card?

_____

5. What interest rate will you pay on new purchases if you default on your card?

_____

6. Why do you think the chart is printed in small type on the back of the letter?

_____

_____

Read this portion of an owner's manual for a cordless telephone. Then answer the questions.

The Battery Pack
_____

If the light does not go on when you put the handset on the base, the battery pack and the AC adapter may not be connected properly. It is also possible that the charging contacts on the base and on the handset need to be cleaned. Do this with an ordinary pencil eraser.

About once a month, discharge the battery fully to maintain its ability to fully recharge. Leaving the handset off the base until the LOW indicator flashes will discharge the battery.

Recharge the battery whenever the LOW indicator flashes. Place the handset on the base for several hours or overnight.

---

1. How can you tell when it is time to recharge the battery?

   A The phone will beep.

   B The light will not go on when you put the handset on the base.

   C You see that a month has gone by since the last recharging.

   D The LOW indicator will flash.

2. How do you discharge the battery completely?

   F Talk on the phone continuously until the battery runs out.

   G Leave the handset off the charger until the LOW indicator flashes.

   H Place the handset on the base for several hours or overnight.

   J Clean the contacts with a pencil eraser.

3. If you put the handset on the base to recharge the battery and the light does not go on, what could be wrong?

   A The battery may not be fully discharged.

   B The battery pack and AC adapter may not be connected properly.

   C The LOW indicator might not have flashed.

   D The antennae may need to be cleaned.

4. If you put the handset on the base to recharge the battery and the light does not go on, what should you do?

   F Clean the connectors with a pencil eraser.

   G Fully discharge the battery.

   H Leave the handset off the base overnight.

   J Wait for the LOW indicator to flash.

Workplace Skill: Use an Employee Direct Deposit Sign-up Document

New employees at a business need to fill out many kinds of consumer documents. These can include sign-up forms for medical insurance, direct paycheck deposit, and 401K savings programs. Employees can elect to join these plans by filling out a form.

Read these portions of the document. Then circle the letter of the answer to each question.

Direct Deposit Sign-up

Worker Only—Complete for Direct Deposit and Sign Below

Bank Account #1	**Bank Account #2**
☐ **Checking** Bank Name _____	☐ **Checking** Bank Name _____
☐ **Savings** Bank Name _____	☐ **Savings** Bank Name _____
I wish to deposit (check one):	**I wish to deposit (check one):**
☐ Remainder of Net Pay	☐ Remainder of Net Pay
☐ _____ % of Net	☐ _____ % of Net
☐ Specific Dollar Amount $ _____	☐ Specific Dollar Amount $ _____
Please attach one of the following for checking or savings accounts (check one):	**Please attach one of the following for checking or savings accounts (check one):**
☐ Voided Check ☐ Deposit Slip	☐ Voided Check ☐ Deposit Slip
☐ Bank Letter (see your local bank representative)	☐ Bank Letter (see your local bank representative)

Worker Signature _____   **Date** _____

By signing above, I am agreeing that I am either the account holder or have the authority of the account holder to authorize my employer to make direct deposits into the named account.

Account Holder Signature _____   **Date** _____

(if worker doesn't have authority to authorize deposits to the account holder's account)

---

1. What should you do to have your paycheck directly deposited into two separate bank accounts?

    A Fill out the left column of the "Worker Only" section of the form.

    B Provide a voided check.

    C Fill out both columns of the "Worker Only" section of the form.

    D Sign on the Account Holder Signature line.

2. In what situation would an account holder's signature be required?

    F if the worker wants to directly deposit into two separate bank accounts

    G if the employee wants to deduct only 20%

    H if the employee does not have a voided check to attach to the form

    J if the worker doesn't have the authority to make deposits to the account holder's account

Write for Work

You are a representative of First Union Bank. A customer has requested a bank letter to accompany her direct deposit sign-up form to certify that she has a bank account at this location. Write a letter in a notebook to authorize her request and give permission to use the direct deposit option of her company.

 Reading Extension

Turn to "Needles That Cure" on page 97 of *Reading Basics Intermediate 1 Reader*. After you have read and/or listened to the article, answer the questions below.

Circle the letter of the answer to each question.

1. What physical problem could an ad for acupuncture offer to cure?

   A heart failure

   B nausea

   C a brain tumor

   D a broken arm

2. How many meridians have Chinese practitioners identified?

   F 5

   G 14

   H 32

   J 1,500

3. How are the needles used in acupuncture believed to work?

   A They allow qi to flow normally by unblocking the body's meridians.

   B They block qi from flowing freely through the body.

   C They cause the patient to focus on a new source of pain.

   D They unclog the body's immune system.

Write the answer to each question.

4. Where might you find the results of Zang-Hee Cho's experiment?

   _____

5. What consumer materials could you use to find out if a certain acupuncturist is good?

   _____

Explore Words

VOWEL COMBINATIONS

The vowel combination *oo* often stands for the long *u* sound. It can also stand for a different sound—the sound you hear in *book*. Vowel combinations *au* and *aw* stand for the sound you hear in the middle of *cause* and at the end of *straw*.

Choose a vowel combination to complete each word. Write it on the line.

1. The accident was not your f_____lt. (oo, au)

2. I will mow the l_____n later. (oo, aw)

3. The plant will bl_____m in the spring. (oo, au)

4. The water in the br_____k is cold. (oo, au)

LONG *i* AND LONG *o*

The letter *i* alone can stand for the long *i* sound, as in the word *mind*. The letter *o* alone can stand for the long *o* sound, as in the word *told*.

Circle the two words in each group that have a long vowel sound.

1. colt   wrong   thinner   kindest   strongest

2. unwind   fonder   blinking   longer   wildness

3. most   invent   fixing   boldness   spinning

4. grinder   cost   risked   scold   thinking

SPELLING: CONTRACTIONS

A contraction is a shorter way to write two words. An apostrophe (') takes the place of letters that are dropped to form the contraction. For example, the contraction *wasn't* stands for the words *was not*. The apostrophe takes the place of the letter *o* in *not*.

Match each pair of words in the left column with the correct contraction in the right column. Write the letter of the answer on the line to the left of the item number. On the line to the right of the contraction, write the letter or letters that were dropped from the word pair.

_____ **1.** he is

_____ **2.** could not

_____ **3.** they are

_____ **4.** we have

_____ **5.** does not

a. we've _____

b. doesn't _____

c. he's _____

d. they're _____

e. couldn't _____

SPELLING: WORD ENDINGS

You can add -ed or -ing to most verbs to change the tense. You can add -er or -est to most short adjectives to compare two or more things. You can add suffixes, such as -able or -ness, to change the part of speech. Sometimes, you have to change the spelling of a base word when you add these endings. Look at these spelling rules:

- To add an ending to a word that ends with silent *e*, drop the final *e* if the ending begins with a vowel and add the ending: for example, *glide/gliding* and *fine/finest*.

- To add an ending to a word that ends with a consonant that comes after one vowel, double the consonant; for example, *hot/hotter* and *jog/jogging*.

- To add an ending to a word that ends with a consonant and *y*, change the *y* to *i*. Then add the ending. For example, look at these words: *try/tried* and *sunny/sunnier*. The rule, however, does not apply when adding -*ing*: for example, *study/studying*.

Add the ending to each word. Write the new word on the line.

1. mad + ness _____

2. hike + ing _____

3. thin + est _____

4. happy + ness _____

5. spin + ing _____

6. help + ful _____

7. carry + ed _____

8. wide + er _____

ACADEMIC VOCABULARY

Knowing these high-frequency words will help you in many school subjects.

consume	to eat, drink, buy, or use up
instructions	directions or orders
purchase	to buy
transfer	to move something from one place to another
annual	yearly

Complete the sentences below using one of the words above.

1. The _____ for programming the phone system were easy to follow.

2. Pedro went online to _____ money from his checking account into his savings account.

3. I _____ fewer sweets now that I have I started my diet.

4. Meli wanted to _____ new speakers for her car.

5. The _____ company picnic is coming up next month.

Lesson 3.4

Recognize Character Traits

People you know or read about and characters in novels or other literary works have character traits. Character traits, or distinguishing qualities, tell you what a character is like—his or her personality, how he or she behaves, and even his or her appearance. Fiction authors use character traits to make subjects seem real. Writers of nonfiction use these same methods to describe real people.

Authors show character traits in a number of ways. Read the list of techniques and the example that follows each technique.

- **Narration:** The author writes how the character looks, states the character's thoughts and feelings, or writes what other characters think about the main character.

    Lu Chu was looking forward to seeing her boyfriend Jim. She was going to give him a birthday gift. She had spent days looking for the perfect present, and she had wrapped it carefully.

- **Dialogue:** The author writes what the character says as well as what other characters say about the main character.

    "I've been waiting for you for *ages*. I have a present for you!" Lu Chu told Jim.

    "I can't wait to see what it is," Jim replied.

- **Action:** The author writes what the character does.

    Lu Chu shifted from one foot to the other. She held the wrapped box out to Jim and began biting her nails as he unwrapped it.

Each method reveals a different character trait that Lu Chu has: thoughtfulness, impatience, and nervousness.

Read the passage. Identify the technique that the author uses to reveal character traits.

> Jeffrey put the headphones over his ears and shoved his hands in his pockets. He turned up the music almost as loud as it would go and walked to the back of the subway car. When other people stood near him, he turned his back to them and pretended to read an advertisement on the wall.

Did you identify the technique as action? In this paragraph, the author describes Jeffrey's actions to show that he is someone who wants to be alone.

Read each passage. On the line, write the phrase from the box that best describes the character.

> ambitious and hardworking
>
> resentful and critical
>
> generous and thoughtful
>
> whiny and dependent

> Theresa pulled the corners of her mouth down into a frown and crossed her arms over her chest. She stamped her foot and asked in a pleading voice, "Can't you stop working and help me? There's no way I can put up all the decorations myself. You know how hard it is to hang streamers."

1. _____

> Kalinda was always complaining about her boss. She said that he was not good at his job, and she always had to complete projects he failed to do. Kalinda was constantly redoing things she thought her boss had done poorly. She wished that everyone would recognize all the hard work she put into her job and stop praising her boss for her work.

2. _____

> When all the employees had gathered in the lunchroom, Arminda brought out a birthday cake for her coworker. Arminda had spent the day before trying to find out the coworker's favorite flavor. Then she had baked the cake and written "Happy Birthday" on it. She was happy when the coworker smiled very widely before he blew out the candles.

3. _____

> Marietta has come a long way during her 10 years at the company. She started working as a receptionist, and before long she became an administrative assistant. Later she transferred to the sales department, and soon she was the company's top salesperson. Within two years, she became a sales manager and has been excelling there ever since. She has always worked hard and set goals for herself. Her current goal is to become vice president of sales.

4. _____

Read each passage. Then write a sentence describing what you have learned about each character's personality.

Tim browsed through his record collection, running his fingers over the thin spines. He had vinyl albums from many different genres: rap, country, rock 'n' roll, classical, rhythm and blues, hip-hop, and jazz. He selected a record and put it on the turntable. He couldn't understand how anyone could tell him that CDs or MP3s sounded as good as vinyl records. Even with all the scratches and pops, he wouldn't trade his collection for anything.

1. _____

Imari is a baker who really enjoys his job. He gets up before the sun rises every morning to make all kinds of breads for the day. He mixes the dough and lets it rise, shapes the bread, and puts it in the oven. He likes the smell of bread while it's baking. Most of all, he likes eating hot, fresh bread right out of the oven. So do his many customers, who think that his bread is the best in town.

2. _____

Vidiraj was always correcting everyone he worked with, pointing out every mistake he thought they made. He corrected people's grammar and pointed out unhealthy food choices at lunch. He said people did not use the office equipment properly and taped detailed instructions on the wall for how to do it better. He never had anything good to say about anyone. Everyone avoided Vidiraj, but he couldn't understand why. He was just trying to help them be better.

3. _____

Chelsea checked the kitchen cabinets and made a list. She wrote down everything she needed and everything that was almost gone. She picked up the stack of sorted and paper-clipped coupons from the counter in one hand and her cloth grocery bags in the other.

4. _____

Read the passage. Then circle the letter of the answer to each question.

The ancient Greeks told a myth of Queen Cassiopeia, wife of the ruler of Ethiopia, who vainly bragged that she was even more beautiful than the sea nymphs. The god of the sea, Poseidon, ruled the nymphs. He heard of Cassiopeia's boast. Poseidon sent a sea monster named Cetus to destroy the coast of Ethiopia.

Cassiopeia and her husband, King Cepheus, had a daughter named Andromeda. The gods told Cassiopeia and King Cepheus that the only way to stop Cetus from destroying the coast was to sacrifice their daughter. Cepheus decided with great sadness that Andromeda must be chained to rocks at the edge of the sea. Just as Cetus was about to kill her, the hero Perseus swooped down from the sky to rescue her. He killed the sea monster and cut Andromeda's chains with his sword.

1. What trait does Queen Cassiopeia have?

   A She is angry.

   B She is conceited.

   C She is humble.

   D She is trustworthy.

2. What trait does Perseus have?

   F He is brave.

   G He is happy.

   H He is lazy.

   J He is cautious.

3. What trait does Poseidon have?

   A He is friendly.

   B He is forgiving.

   C He is vengeful.

   D He is careless.

4. What technique does the writer use to show both Perseus's and Poseidon's characters?

   F narration

   G dialogue

   H comments from other people about him

   J action

Workplace Skill: Compare Character Traits in a Planning Document

A planning document describes how to do or accomplish something. Workplace planning depends upon the needs of the organization. The human resources manager of a company asked two supervisors separately to develop a planning document that would help supervisors improve employee morale and job satisfaction.

Read the two planning documents. Then circle the letter of the answer to each question.

Planning Document: Improve Employee Morale

submitted by Toni Green

1. Ask employees: Get employee input on the causes and solutions of bad morale.
2. Show concern: Supervisors should make it clear that they care about employees' feelings.
3. Set goals: Set goals that are mutually acceptable so that employees know what is expected by their supervisors.
4. Provide positive feedback: Give regular verbal appreciation for employees' efforts.

Planning Document: Improve Employee Morale

submitted by Michael Harrington

1. Establish a suggestion box. Employees can submit their concerns and complaints.
2. Help employees wake up. Offer free brewed coffee to help employees stay awake and alert.
3. Start an employee appreciation day. Provide free pizza and soda to all employees once a month.
4. Help relieve stress. Schedule a workshop conducted by a stress-management teacher so employees can learn and practice good stress-management skills.

---

1. Based on her planning document, Toni Green's management style values

    A   personal interaction with her employees.

    B   the safety of her employees.

    C   supervisors who avoid showing appreciation.

    D   employees who solve their own workplace concerns.

2. Based on his planning document, Michael Harrington's management style values

    F   the importance of setting goals for employees.

    G   a communal and positive workplace environment.

    H   employees who are punctual and alert.

    J   supervisors who provide positive role models for employees.

Write for Work

Your supervisor has asked you to prepare a planning document on how to keep the lunchroom and refrigerator clean and neat. Think about what steps employees can take when using the lunchroom each day. Think about what steps employees could take each week to keep the lunchroom clean. Write your planning document in a notebook.

  Reading Extension

Turn to "Hanging from a Cliff" on page 105 of *Reading Basics Intermediate 1 Reader*. After you have read and/or listened to the article, answer the questions below.

Circle the letter of the answer to each question.

1. Reread paragraph 1. What technique does the author use to show Young's character?

   A dialogue

   B action

   C narration

   D comments by other characters about him

2. Reread paragraph 10. What technique does the author use to show Muir's character?

   F dialogue

   G action

   H narration

   J comments by other characters about him

3. Which character traits best describe S. Hall Young?

   A incapable and clumsy

   B gutsy and optimistic

   C timid and fearful

   D whiny and childish

Write the answer to each question.

4. What are some character traits that Muir exhibits?

   _____

5. What are some techniques the author uses to show Muir's character traits?

   _____

Explore Words

r-CONTROLLED VOWELS

When a vowel is followed by the letter *r*, the vowel stands for a sound that is not short or long. You can hear the *r*-controlled vowel sound in the words *cart*, *herd*, *shirt*, *torn*, and *turn*. Notice that *er*, *ir*, and *ur* are different spellings for the same vowel sound.

Say the first word in each row and notice the *r*-controlled vowel sound. Then circle the word in the rest of the row that has the same *r*-controlled vowel sound.

1. carbon   disturb   catfish   target
2. storage   ageless   hornet   stringy
3. birdfeed   curtain   bringing   braided

VOWEL COMBINATIONS

Some vowel combinations stand for more than one sound. The vowel pair *ea* can stand for short *e (bread)*, long *e (treat)*, or long *a (break)*. The vowel combination *ey* can stand for long *a (they)* or long *e (key)*. The vowel pair *ie* can stand for long *e (chief, carried)* or long *i (tie, replied)*.

Read each sentence or ask your teacher to read it. Name the sound of the underlined vowel combination. The first item is done for you.

1. The office suppl<u>ie</u>s are in the small room.   _____*long i*_____

2. What were the results of the voter surv<u>ey</u>?   _____

3. She was rel<u>ie</u>ved that the test was not hard.   _____

4. The fever made Karina weak and unst<u>ea</u>dy.   _____

SUFFIXES -*y*, -*en*

A suffix is a word part that can be added to the end of many words. Adding a suffix changes the meaning of the word. The suffix -*y* means "characterized by" or "like," and -*en* means "to become" or "made of."

Add the suffix -*y* or -*en* to each word to make it match the meaning. Write the new word.

1. made of wood   wood   _____

2. characterized by rain   rain   _____

3. like oil   oil   _____

4. become weak   weak   _____

MULTIPLE-MEANING WORDS

Some words have more than one meaning. For example, a *cap* is a type of hat. Used another way, a *cap* can also be a cover for a bottle. You can use context clues—other words in the same or nearby sentences—to figure out which meaning is intended.

Use context clues in each sentence to help you understand the meaning of the underlined word. Circle the letter of the intended meaning.

1. The senator will not serve the rest of his <u>term</u>.
   a. a limited period of time
   b. a word or phrase

2. Cassie <u>declined</u> the invitation to the party.
   a. refused
   b. became worse

3. You can cast a shadow if you <u>block</u> the sun.
   a. a piece of hard material with flat surfaces
   b. get in the way of

4. The last <u>batter</u> hit a home run.
   a. a person who hits a ball with a bat
   b. a mixture of flour, eggs, and milk

5. Eiji will not be able to go because of <u>poor</u> health.
   a. without money or resources
   b. bad

6. The doctor <u>combed</u> through the reports for clues.
   a. arranged hair or fur with a special instrument
   b. looked closely

7. Use a rubber <u>band</u> to keep the dollar bills together.
   a. a group of musicians
   b. an elastic strip used for binding

8. What is your favorite <u>subject</u> in school?
   a. a branch of knowledge
   b. a citizen in a kingdom

ACADEMIC VOCABULARY

Knowing these high-frequency words will help you in many school subjects.

characters	the people in a fictional work
traits	qualities that make people special
exhibit	to show or display outwardly
distinguish	to perceive or recognize a difference
genres	categories of art, music, or literature

Complete the sentences below using one of the words above.

1. The artist hoped to _____ some work in a local gallery.

2. The two major _____ in the play were resourceful and cunning.

3. The kitten's white spot made him easy to _____ from his littermates.

4. Happiness and cheer were not _____ that the man possessed.

5. Drama and poetry are my favorite literary _____.

Lesson 3.5

Identify Fact and Opinion

When you write, you may use a mix of facts and opinions. You can prove or disprove a fact. A fact could be a specific date, a statistic, a historical event, or other information that can be tested and proved. An opinion gives a person's viewpoint on or judgment about an issue, event, or other topic. You can agree or disagree with an opinion. An opinion cannot be proven. Opinions can be stated directly or implied. Many types of writing combine fact and opinion to convey a writer's viewpoint. Read the examples.

> Fact: Joe DiMaggio had a hitting streak of 56 games.
> Opinion: Joe DiMaggio was a better baseball player than Lou Gehrig.

The first statement is a fact. You can look in an encyclopedia or a sports statistics book or on the Internet to check how long DiMaggio's hitting streak lasted. The second statement is an opinion. It can't be proven. You can agree that DiMaggio was the better ball player, or you can disagree and think Gehrig was more talented. Keep in mind that an incorrect fact is still a fact. If you said that DiMaggio's hitting streak was 67 games, it would be a false fact. Read the examples.

> False fact: George Washington was the seventh president of the United States.
> Opinion: George Washington was the best American president in history.

Read the following statements. Then underline the sentences that state facts and circle the sentences that state opinions.

1. This shirt is made of 100 percent cotton.
2. Cotton is the best material for T-shirts.
3. Everyone should own a nice white T-shirt.
4. This shirt is also available in black.

You should have underlined sentences 1 and 4. These statements are facts. They can be proven. You might look at the label of the shirt to prove the first statement and check a catalog to prove the fourth statement. You should have circled sentences 2 and 3. These sentences are opinions and cannot be proven. The words *best* in the second sentence and *should* in the third sentence signal to the reader that these are opinions.

Decide whether each statement is a fact or an opinion. Write each statement in the appropriate column in the graphic organizer.

The Great Pyramid of Giza is about 450 feet high.

A pyramid is one of the most inspiring sights on Earth.

Ancient Egypt had one of the greatest civilizations of all time.

Egyptians used papyrus, a form of paper made from a tall water reed.

Egyptian pyramids served as royal tombs.

When a pharaoh died, he was buried with many treasures.

A mummy is spooky looking.

Egyptian bodies were mummified, or preserved in salt, dried out, and wrapped in cloth.

The modern way of preserving bodies is better than the ancient Egyptian method.

Fact	Opinion

Read the statements. Write *F* beside each fact and *O* beside each opinion. For each fact, write the name of the source or sources you could use to prove it. Choose among these sources: atlas, newspaper, or encyclopedia. Some items may have more than one answer.

_____ **1.** Alaska is the largest state in the United States.

_____

_____ **2.** Common turkeys are native to North America.

_____

_____ **3.** Wild turkeys are really funny looking.

_____

_____ **4.** The eagle is a cruel bird.

_____

_____ **5.** The colonial period was the most exciting era in U.S. history.

_____

_____ **6.** The Revolutionary War was fought between 1775 and 1783.

_____

_____ **7.** The city's annual celebration of Independence Day had a turnout of 4,000 people this year.

_____

_____ **8.** Thomas Jefferson was the most brilliant of the colonial leaders.

_____

_____ **9.** The country of Kenya is located on the continent of Africa.

_____

_____ **10.** The New England Patriots are the best team in the National Football League.

_____

_____ **11.** Japan had a 7.4 magnitude earthquake yesterday.

_____

Circle the letter of the answer to each question.

1. Which of the following statements is a fact?

   A Wild cats are the most graceful animals in the world.

   B Cheetahs live in parts of Africa.

   C Jaguars are sneaky.

   D The lion is truly the king of the beasts.

2. Which of the following statements is an opinion?

   F Some people still go to see movies at a theater.

   G Charlie Chaplin was one of the founders of the production company United Artists.

   H There is nothing more exciting than seeing a first-run film on the big screen.

   J Many people can watch movies at home on their televisions or on their computers.

3. Which of the following is a fact?

   A Puerto Rico should become the 51st state.

   B Puerto Rico is a wonderful vacation destination.

   C Puerto Rico offers everything a traveler could want.

   D Puerto Rico is an island.

4. Which of the following is an opinion?

   F California has a large population compared to Utah.

   G California is a more influential state than New York.

   H California is known as "The Golden State."

   J Many technology companies are located in California.

5. Which of the following is a fact?

   A *West Side Story* was written to be a modern version of *Romeo and Juliet*.

   B Both stories are equally sad.

   C The composer of the music for *West Side Story* was a genius.

   D Natalie Wood was perfect as Maria in the film version of *West Side Story*.

6. Which of the following is an opinion?

   F Daylight saving time was created to save energy used for lighting.

   G People move clocks an hour ahead in the spring.

   H Railroad company executives created the idea of standard time in 1883.

   J We couldn't exist without standard time in our busy society.

Workplace Skill: Distinguish between Fact and Opinion in a Business Ad

Many businesses rely on advertisements (or *ads*) to sell their products. Advertisements are persuasive messages meant to convince you to buy something, think something, or do something. Ads are often a combination of fact and opinion.

Read the ad. Then circle the letter of the answer to each question.

StormStand Homes

Would Your Home Be Safe in a Hurricane? Probably NOT!

If you live in an area where hurricanes are common, your house is probably not strong enough to withstand strong winds—not unless it's a StormStand home!

StormStand homes have survived Hurricane Andrew in Florida and Hurricane Katrina along the Gulf Coast. Each attractive StormStand home is designed to resist strong winds and rain. Our trained builders combine modern engineering and design with a classic post-and-beam building system to create homes that are strong fortresses against dangerous storms. We create our houses on stilts or pilings off the ground so that winds flow under, over, and around them.

No home is completely storm proof, but StormStand is as close as you can get.

Ask Anyone!

1. Which information in the ad is a fact?

   A StormStand homes are attractive.

   B StormStand is as close as you can get to being storm proof.

   C StormStand homes are raised off the ground.

   D Your home is probably not strong enough to stand up to strong winds.

2. What is the purpose of this statement: "Would your home be safe in a hurricane? Probably NOT!"?

   F to convince you that you are not safe without a StormStand home

   G to persuade you not to live in hurricane zones

   H to convince you to go out during a hurricane

   J to show that StormStand homes are not safe

Write for Work

You work in the advertising department of a major department store. Your store is having a sale on winter coats. In a notebook, create an ad for the upcoming sale. Use a combination of fact and opinion in the ad. Be sure to use appropriate persuasive language.

 Reading Extension

Turn to "Killer Bees" on page 113 of *Reading Basics Intermediate 1 Reader*. After you have read and/or listened to the article, answer the questions below.

Circle the letter of the answer to each question.

1. Which of the following is an opinion?
   - **A**   Killer bees are more aggressive when they are disturbed.
   - **B**   It takes European bees 19 seconds to get irritated enough to sting.
   - **C**   European bees make better honey than killer bees.
   - **D**   Killer bees are a fact of life for people in warm states.

2. Which of the following is a fact?
   - **F**   Killer bees can kill a human being.
   - **G**   It is good that killer bees die out in cold climates.
   - **H**   It was a bad plan to bring European bees to Latin America.
   - **J**   Honey is so delicious that it's worth the trouble the killer bees have caused.

3. Which of the following statements is an opinion?
   - **A**   Today killer bees are a fact of life in Texas.
   - **B**   Killer bees still love hot weather.
   - **C**   Whenever they stray to colder regions, they die.
   - **D**   That's good news for anyone who likes to mow the lawn in peace.

Write the answer to each question.

4. What is one fact you learned from the article about killer bees?

   _____

5. What is your opinion of killer bees?

   _____

Explore Words

CONSONANT PAIRS

When *sc* is followed by *a, o,* or *u,* you can hear the sounds of *s* and hard *c,* as in *scoop.* When *sc* is followed by *e, i,* or *y,* the *c* is silent, as in *scent.* When *mb* appears in a one-syllable word, the *b* is silent, as in *thumb.* In many two-syllable words, you can hear the sounds of *m* and *b,* as in *lumber.*

Say each word. Then circle the words in which *mb* and *sc* stand for only one sound.

1. crumb

2. scissor

3. timber

4. scale

5. stumble

6. descend

SPELLING: POSSESSIVES

Possessive words show that something belongs to one or more than one person. Singular possessive words include an apostrophe followed by *s* ('s). For example, the apartment of your friend is *your friend's apartment.* Most plural possessive words include an *s* followed by an apostrophe (s'). For example, the apartment where two or more of your friends live is *your friends' apartment.*

Circle the correct way to form each possessive.

1. the drums your son has

2. the party that my sisters gave

3. the maps belonging to the driver

4. the children of my uncles

your son's drums

my sister's party

the driver's maps

my uncle's children

your sons' drums

my sisters' party

the drivers' maps

my uncles' children

SYLLABLES

Words consist of one or more syllables, and each syllable has one vowel sound. Vowel pairs such as *ai* and *ow* stay together in one syllable (<u>ai</u> / ment, yel / <u>low</u>). R-controlled vowels, such as *ar, er, ir, or,* and *ur,* also stay together in one syllable (<u>car</u> / ton). Consonant + *le* syllables usually appear at the end of a word (jun / g<u>le</u>).

Combine each pair of syllables to make a word. Write the word on the line. If the first syllable in the word has an *r*-controlled vowel sound, circle it. If it has a long vowel sound, underline it. The first item has been done for you.

1. bea   gle   *beagle*

2. tur   tle   _____

3. var   nish   _____

4. main   ly   _____

5. han   dle   _____

6. skir   mish   _____

BASE WORDS

Many words in English consist of base words to which prefixes, suffixes, and other endings have been added. Recognizing word parts can help you read and understand longer words. Read the following words and their word parts.

Word	Prefix	Base Word	Suffix/Ending
unstoppable	un	stop	able
redoing	re	do	ing
subcontracted	sub	contract	ed

Read each word. Circle any prefixes, suffixes, or other endings. Then write the base word on the line.

1. largest _____

2. previewing _____

3. unlucky _____

4. subleased _____

5. undependable _____

6. prestamped _____

7. unhelpful _____

8. resellable _____

ACADEMIC VOCABULARY

Knowing these high-frequency words will help you in many school subjects.

fact   a historical date, a statistic, a specific action, or other information that can be tested and proven

opinion   what someone thinks or believes about something

prove   to demonstrate the existence, truth, or validity of something

viewpoint   a particular attitude or way of thinking about something

signal   to indicate the existence or occurrence of something

Complete the sentences below using one of the words above.

1. Rafaela's _____ was that the musicians were not very good.

2. It was easy to _____ that the article was accurate.

3. Julia checked the _____ in the almanac.

4. Shalisa tried to see the situation from her sister's _____.

5. The bell rang to _____ that dinner was ready.

Lesson 3.6

Use Indexes

Most reference books have indexes at the back to help you find information quickly. The index of a book lists names, topics, and important terms that are mentioned in the book. Each page where an item appears is listed. Entries are listed in alphabetical order, and people are listed by last name first.

Sometimes a book has a lot of information about one particular subject. In that case, the index also lists subentries. Examine the index from a guidebook about New Orleans. You can scan the page to find the topic you need. For example, if you wanted to find information about bed-and-breakfast inns, you would look under *Accommodations* and find the subentry for *bed-and-breakfast inns*.

Index

Accommodations	Boat tours, 121
bed-and-breakfast inns, 73–74	Bridges, 288–289
camping, 70–72	Bus tours, 130–131
hotels, 75–76	Cajun Country, 160–173
map, 3–4	food, 165–166
Airport, 35	map of, 166
Air travel, 52	music, 171–173
Aquarium, 164	Campgrounds, 70–72
Avery Island, 235	Car rentals, 99–100
Babysitters, 29	Children's activities, 214–220
Baton Rouge, 151–152, 245–246	Cooking lessons, 200–203

Use the index above to answer the following questions.

On what page would you find information about the aquarium?
If you are traveling with children, which two entries might be helpful?
What topic is discussed on page 121?

You can find information about the aquarium on page 164. If you are traveling with children, you might want to review the entries for babysitters and for children's activities. Boat tours are discussed on page 121.

Some magazines give information in an index at the back of the magazine. For example, in a food magazine, the index lists where to find recipes.

Read the index. Then answer the questions.

Recipes

Fish and Shellfish

Corn-fried Fish, 74

Salmon with Dill, 52

Scallops with Lime, 64

Shrimp and Garlic, 38

Salads

Asparagus with Parmesan, 99

Cucumber and Walnut, 40

Pepper and Tomato, 19

Spicy Chicken, 34

Warm Bean, 93

Soups

Flat Noodle, 83

Garlic Chive, 54

Mushroom and Herb, 22

Vegetable Side Dishes

Green Beans with Chives, 24

Potato Curry, 37

Tomatoes with Cheese, 28

1. How many soup recipes appear in this issue? _____

2. Which recipe uses dill as a main ingredient? _____

3. On what page would you find a recipe that uses potatoes as a main ingredient?

_____

4. Are there any recipes with *carrots* in the name? If there are, name them.

_____

5. How many entries have *chives* in the recipe name? _____

6. Which recipe has *chicken* in its name? _____

7. On what page would you find the chicken recipe? _____

8. Are there any recipes that use tomatoes as a main ingredient? If there are, name them.

_____

9. In what order are the recipes listed in each category? _____

Some indexes give additional information. They might indicate if an entry includes a picture, a diagram, or another feature.

Read the index about plants. Then decide if each statement following the index is true or false. Circle the answer. If the statement is false, explain why.

Index

salvia (plant), 32
sassafras (tree), how to identify, 131
sea lettuce (plant), 75, *picture*
seasons
    desert, 98, *picture*, 99
    mountains, 102, *picture*, 103
    northern forest, 95
    woodland, 87, *picture*, 88

seaweed (plant), 207
sequoia (tree), 175, *picture*
silver fir (tree), 220, *picture*
skunk cabbage (plant), 22, *picture*
snap bean (plant), 72, *picture*

1. Seaweed is a plant.

    true   false

_____

2. In this book, a picture of a silver fir tree is found on page 32.

    true   false

_____

3. This book explains how to identify a sassafras tree.

    true   false

_____

4. You can find a picture of a northern forest on page 95.

    true   false

_____

5. Skunk cabbage is an insect.

    true   false

_____

Read the index. Then circle the letter of the answer to each question.

> **Index**
>
> Paris (France)
>
>   Eiffel Tower, 120, *with picture*
>
> Parthenon (Athens), 130; 131, *with picture*
>
> Pearl Harbor
>
>   monument, 110, *with picture*
>
> Pennsylvania, 186
>
>   Liberty Bell, 187, *with picture*
>
> Peru, 215
>
> Pisa (Italy)
>
>   Leaning Tower, 163, *with picture*
>
> Plymouth Rock, 198, *with picture*
>
> pyramid (Egyptian tomb), 19, *with picture;* 154

1. On what page would you find a picture of the Parthenon?

  A 130

  B 131

  C 110

  D 163

2. Which entry does NOT have a picture?

  F Pearl Harbor

  G Peru

  H Leaning Tower of Pisa

  J Liberty Bell

3. According to the index, what is a general definition of a pyramid?

  A a tower

  B a bell

  C a tomb

  D a rock

4. On what page would you find a picture of the Liberty Bell?

  F 187

  G 120

  H 110

  J 198

5. What would you find on page 110?

  A information about pyramids

  B information about Peru

  C a picture of the Pearl Harbor monument

  D a picture of the Liberty Bell

6. On what page would you find information about Plymouth Rock?

  F 187

  G 131

  H 215

  J 198

Workplace Skill: Use Indexes to Locate Information

At work you may need to use reference books, instruction manuals, or guides to find information. Many of these materials have indexes. Instead of thumbing through the material, you can use an index to find specific information quickly.

Read this section of an index from an employee handbook. Then circle the letter of the answer to each question.

Employee Handbook Index

B		**C**	
Benefits		Care of Equipment and Supplies	32
Bonus Plan	14	Code of Ethical Conduct	3
Flexible Spending Account Plan	16	Company Mission Statement	2
Group Medical Insurance	11	Compensatory Time Off	8
Holiday Pay	8	Computer and Electronics	
Paid Time Off	11	Communications Policy	
401K and Profit-Sharing Plan	16	Computer Use Guidelines	22
Business Expenses		Mobile Phone Use Guidelines	22
Expense Reimbursement Form	26	Conduct at Clients' Offices	29
Reimbursement Guidelines	27	Confidential and Proprietary Information	5

1. You have attended a business conference and need to be reimbursed for your expenses. On which page would you find a copy of the form?

   A   26

   B   27

   C   29

   D   5

2. You have a client meeting at the client's office. Which category would you use to find specific information on how the company wants employees to behave?

   F   Company Mission Statement

   G   Confidential and Proprietary Information

   H   Conduct at Clients' Offices

   J   Business Expenses

3. You want to plan a trip around Thanksgiving. On which page could you find more information?

   A   14

   B   8

   C   11

   D   5

4. One of the copiers is broken. Which category would you use to figure out what to do next?

   F   Care of Equipment and Supplies

   G   Bonus Plan

   H   Computer Use Guidelines

   J   Mobile Phone Use Guidelines

Write for Work

A coworker has asked you how to fix a problem with the fax machine. In a notebook, write a note or e-mail message telling your coworker how to find the information he or she needs in the index of the fax machine manual.

Workplace Extension

Ryan is going to take the GED test in a few months. He is starting to think about what his next steps should be after he gets his GED credential. He has always been interested in how things work and in taking apart and rebuilding computers and other electronic products. He found the following information on the Internet.

Electronics Manufacturing

The computer and electronics manufacturing industry produces computers, communications equipment, and similar electronic products. About a third of employees in this field are production workers. About half of those are assemblers. Their job is to place components on circuit boards or assemble and connect the various parts of electronic devices.

Electronic equipment assemblers are responsible for putting together products such as computers and appliances, phone equipment, and even missile control systems.

Circle the letter of the answer to the question.

1. If Ryan is interested in working in electronics manufacturing, what is one of the first things he should do?

   A enroll in an electrical engineering course at his state college

   B go to a factory and talk to as many workers as he can

   C find out what the educational requirements and qualifications are for electronics manufacturing

   D find out how much money he can make working in electronics manufacturing

Write the answer to the question.

2. What other jobs might Ryan explore to use his skills and interests in the field of electronics?

   _____

   _____

   _____

Explore Words

The schwa sound is the sound *uh*. You can hear the schwa sound at the beginning and at the end of the word *aroma*. Every vowel can stand for the schwa sound, as in *above*, *barrel*, *pencil*, *gallop*, and *circus*. The schwa sound is heard in unstressed syllables. For example, say these words: *random, postal, people,* and *lotus*. The second syllable in each word is unstressed and contains the schwa sound.

Say the words aloud or ask your teacher to say them. Then circle the two words in each row that contain the schwa sound.

1. pupil	secret	ladies	creepy
2. cupid	lately	invade	regal
3. seaweed	translate	afraid	freedom
4. excite	unit	female	frozen

SYLLABLES

The following groups of syllables are scrambled. Put each group in order to form a three-syllable word. Then write the word. The first item has been done for you.

1. sta un ble   *unstable*

2. lief dis be   _____

3. spect ed in   _____

4. glim ing mer   _____

5. dle re kin   _____

6. ap pre prove   _____

PREFIXES *uni-, bi-, tri-*

Some prefixes have meanings that indicate number. For example, the prefix *uni-* means "one," the prefix *bi-* means "two," and the prefix *tri-* means "three."

Write the prefix *uni-*, *bi-*, or *tri-* on the line to make a word with the meaning given.

1. A _____ angle is a shape that has three angles.

2. A _____ athlon is an athletic competition consisting of three events.

3. _____ lingual means "able to speak two languages."

4. A _____ cycle is a type of cycle with one wheel.

5. _____ focals are eyeglasses that have lenses with two parts.

Plural nouns name more than one person, place, or thing. Use the following rules:

- To make most nouns plural, add -s to the end of the word (*student* / *students*).
- To form the plural of words that end with *s*, *ss*, *sh*, *x*, or *ch*, add -es (*boss* / *bosses*).
- For words that end in *y*, change the *y* to *i* and add -es (*penny* / *pennies*).
- For most words that end with *f*, *ff*, or *fe*, add -s to form the plural (*chiefs*, *spoofs*, *staffs*).
- For some words that end with *f*, change the final *f* to *ves* (*half* / *halves*; *wolf* / *wolves*). Use a dictionary if you're not sure.
- For some words that end in -*fe*, first change the *f* to *v*, and then add -s (*wife* / *wives*).

Write the plural form of each word on the line.

1. giraffe _____

2. lady _____

3. shelf _____

4. class _____

5. bench _____

6. scruff _____

7. self _____

8. strawberry _____

9. tax _____

10. proof _____

Knowing these high-frequency words will help you in many school subjects.

index   an alphabetical list of names, topics, and important terms that are mentioned in a book and each page where an item appears

subject   what a certain text is about

discuss   to talk about

order   the arrangement of things in relation to each other

scan   to look quickly through something in order to find a particular thing

Complete the sentences below using one of the words above.

1. The _____ of the book is dog training.

2. Makoto put the books in _____ according to the publication date.

3. At dinner, Estrella didn't want to _____ the problem with anyone.

4. Emere had to _____ the list several times before she found the name she needed.

5. Jamaica looked in the _____ to find out what page the topic was on.

Unit 3 Review

Predict Outcomes

When you read, clues in the text can help you figure out what will happen next. You notice details in the text and then think about your own experiences. You can use this information to predict an outcome. You can make predictions at any time during your reading. You can adjust your predictions as you read.

Identify Cause and Effect

You ask *why* when you want to know the cause of something. When you read, you may learn about some things that make other things happen. The event that happens is the effect. The reason it happens is the cause.

Some of the words and phrases that signal that a cause-and-effect relationship is present are *as a result, due to, so, because, if, then, therefore, consequently, since,* and *thus.*

Understand Consumer Materials

We are all consumers. When we buy products and services, we need to know important information about them in order to use them safely. We might also want to know what they contain. Labels on packages, advertisements, and product instructions are examples of consumer materials.

Recognize Character Traits

People in real life and characters in fiction have character traits. These traits include the person or character's behavior patterns, physical appearance, and personality. Authors show character traits through narration, dialogue, and action. The author may also tell what other people think or say about the character or person.

Identify Fact and Opinion

Facts can be proved. You can look them up or check them in some way. Opinions tell what someone believes or thinks. Facts can be true or false. Opinions are neither true nor false. When you read, it is important to separate facts from opinions.

Use Indexes

The index of a book lists names, topics, and important terms that are covered in the book. Entries are listed alphabetically at the back of the book. Each entry lists the page number(s) on which the topic is mentioned. You can look in the index in order to find something you are looking for in the book.

Unit 3 Assessment

Read each passage. Then circle the letter of the answer to each question.

> Tariq has always dreamed of owning a motorcycle. Instead of taking the bus to work, Tariq walks most of the time because he is saving money to buy a used motorcycle. He reads motorcycle magazines and also follows a motorcycle blog on the Internet. He knows exactly what model he wants and what color he prefers. He has figured out the accessories he will need, such as a helmet, a jacket, and sturdy boots. He has even looked into the cost of motorcycle insurance. One day he sees an ad in the newspaper, and he realizes that the exact motorcycle he wants is for sale at a good price.

1. What do you predict will happen next?

   A Tariq will call the person who is selling the motorcycle.

   B Tariq will decide he doesn't want the motorcycle after all.

   C Tariq's friends will buy the motorcycle for him.

   D Tariq will change his mind about what color he likes.

2. Tariq's behavior indicates that he is a _____ person.

   F lazy

   G shy

   H curious

   J determined

> People used to make fire by rubbing two sticks together. The rubbing motion created friction, and the friction created heat and sparks. The sparks caused any burnable materials next to the sticks to catch fire. Matches work in the same way but faster. Match tips are coated with chemicals that spark and burn easily. Burning matches have a nasty odor. When a match is struck against a surface, the friction makes the chemicals spark. The spark then reacts quickly with the chemicals to make a flame. The flame can then burn all the way down the length of the matchstick.

3. The spark needed to start a fire is an effect caused by

   A a flame.

   B chemicals.

   C friction.

   D sticks.

4. Which statement below expresses an opinion?

   F Match tips are coated with chemicals.

   G Burning matches have a nasty odor.

   H Matches work in the same way as rubbing two sticks together because of the heat caused by friction.

   J Matches light quickly because they are coated with chemicals.

Until the late 1800s most of the rice eaten around the world was brown, the natural color of rice. A new method for processing rice was introduced, which resulted in white grains. The method involved scraping off the outer brown layers of the rice grains. White rice looks prettier than brown rice. When people switched from brown rice to white, many of them got sick with a serious disease called beriberi. After extensive research, scientists discovered that the white rice was missing an important vitamin. This vitamin was contained in the outer brown shell of the rice. Scientists learned that beriberi results from lack of thiamine, or vitamin B_1, in the daily diet of the people who had switched to white rice.

5. Which sentence expresses an opinion?

A Most of the rice eaten around the world was brown until the late 1800s.

B White rice looks prettier than brown rice.

C A vitamin was contained in the outer brown shell of the rice.

D The method for processing rice involved scraping off the outer brown layers.

6. Which sentence explains the cause of beriberi?

F Extensive research uncovered the cause.

G A machine scraped off the outer brown layers of the rice.

H Beriberi results from lack of thiamine, or vitamin B_1, in the daily diet.

J Many people got sick with a serious disease called beriberi.

Today is Narisha's 21st birthday. She's been waiting impatiently for this day, so she is surprised, and a little hurt, that no one has suggested any big plans to help her celebrate. After all, it's a special occasion! Her parents did call the day before, but they simply said, "Happy birthday, Dear. Your gift will be coming late." She found a card from her roommate Susan this morning, but there was no gift with it. In fact, Susan even mentioned casually that she wouldn't be home until late tonight. "I won't even have a cake," Narisha thought to herself in dismay. After work, Narisha gets off the bus as usual and climbs the stairs to her apartment with a heavy heart. But strangely, just as she unlocks the apartment door, she thinks she hears whispering inside.

7. What probably happens next?

A Narisha has a quiet dinner and goes to bed early.

B Narisha's friends and family jump out and yell "Surprise!"

C Narisha makes up her mind to celebrate by herself.

D Narisha's roommate brings her a cake when she comes home later.

8. Narisha's family and friends can be described as

F cruel.

G thoughtful.

H forgetful.

J boring.

Read the index. Then circle the letter of the answer to each question.

Index

caffeine, 126, 228

circulation, 36, 66, 120

coughing reflex, 200

defibrillator, 266

diabetes, 216

diet, 315, 356

---

9. Where would you add an entry for calcium?

  A between *caffeine* and *circulation*

  B before the entry for caffeine

  C between *circulation* and *coughing reflex*

  D after the entry for coughing reflex

10. What page discusses the causes of coughing?

  F page 36

  G page 200

  H page 266

  J page 356

Study the consumer information. Then circle the letter of the answer to each question.

Dial Anywhere Calling Plan

Calling Plan	This Plan Includes:
$39.99 per month	500 anytime minutes*, $0.20 per text message, no Web access
$42.99 per month	700 anytime minutes*, $0.20 per text message, no Web access
$45.99 per month	500 anytime minutes*, unlimited text messages, no Web access
$49.99 per month	500 anytime minutes*, $0.20 per text message, unlimited Web access
$52.99 per month	300 anytime minutes*, unlimited text messages, unlimited Web access

*Each extra minute is $0.25. All plans include unlimited minutes on nights and weekends.

---

11. Your phone bill shows that you average 450 minutes and 150 text messages per month. You don't want Web access. Which plan do you choose?

  A $39.99 per month

  B $45.99 per month

  C $49.99 per month

  D $42.99 per month

12. You use 450 minutes per month on the weekends, but only 300 minutes per month during the week. You send many text messages and use Web access on your phone. Which plan do you choose?

  F $39.99 per month

  G $52.99 per month

  H $49.99 per month

  J $42.99 per month

Read the vacation policy. Then circle the letter of the answer to each question.

Policy and Procedures Manual

SECTION 4d: VACATION POLICY—PART 2

You deserve a rest! We encourage everyone to take all accumulated vacation time as described in Section 4c. In this section we explain the reason for submitting requests welll in advance. We also describe the possible consequence of not respecting this time frame.

As you know, this company has won many productivity awards in our industry. This is largely due to the pod concept, first developed by our founder. We are each members of a cross-functional pod, or team. Within the pod, we share common goals and responsibilities. Since our contracts are with government agencies, there is no leeway in the production schedules. **When a member is not available, the absence affects the other members of the pod. This puts an extra burden on each one and potentially jeopardizes the schedule.**

Therefore, elective absences (as opposed to sick days) must be planned for and approved in advance. Specifically, you must submit your vacation request **in writing** within the following time frames:

• one week in advance for a one-day absence

• two weeks in advance for a one-week absence

• one month in advance for a two-week absence

The request must be approved first by your supervisor and then submitted to the human resources department. Your supervisor will make every effort to accommodate your request. However, the pod needs a minimum number of members to accomplish its goals, so at times it may not be possible to grant your request. We do not want you to be disappointed. **Please plan ahead.**

13. This company expects its employees to exhibit a spirit of

   A   collaboration.

   B   punctuality.

   C   politeness.

   D   playfulness.

14. Which statement from the passage is an opinion?

   F   We are each members of a cross-functional pod.

   G   This company has won many productivity awards.

   H   You deserve a rest!

   J   Our contracts are with government agencies.

15. What is the most likely outcome of not following the vacation policy?

   A   The company will lose a government contract.

   B   You may get extra vacation time.

   C   Your vacation request will not be granted.

   D   You will have to work more hours.

16. What might cause the company to refuse your vacation request?

   F   asking for a two-week vacation one week before you want to leave

   G   giving your request in writing to your supervisor

   H   going to your supervisor before human resources

   J   asking for a one-day vacation one week in advance

Read the index for a factory orientation handbook. Then circle the letter of the answer to each question.

```
                              Index
cafeteria                                health and safety
     hours of operation, 14                   defibrillator, 21
     location (see floor plan)                fire exits, 21
     menu access (see Web services)           first aid, 21
company headquarters                          hazardous materials, 21
     address, 2                          human resources, 6
     directions, 2                       management team, 6
complaints                               organization, 6
     how to file, 7                      part-time employees, 15
contract employees, 13–15, 19            promotions, 25
elevators, 3                             restrooms (see floor plan)
employees                                security card, 14
     department heads, 32                tech support
     e-mail addresses, 33                     computers, 9–12
     names, 33                                copiers and printers, 13–15
     telephone extensions (see telephones)  telephones
floor plan, 4–5                               office phone extensions, 24
full-time employees                           office phone instructions, 23
     hours, 14                           time cards, 15
     overtime pay, 14                    union representatives, 38
```

17. Where would you add an entry for time off?

   A before the entry for tech support

   B after the entry for telephones

   C after the entry for time cards

   D after the entry for union representative

18. On what page would you look for directions to the company headquarters?

   F page 2

   G page 6

   H page 11

   J page 12

19. How would you locate the nearest restroom?

   A Look under health and safety.

   B Ask the receptionist.

   C Look under company headquarters.

   D Look under floor plan.

20. What page would help you find out how to get overtime pay?

   F page 6

   G page 14

   H page 18

   J page 22

Circle the letter of the answer to each question.

21. Which word does not contain a silent consonant?

    A gnaw

    B write

    C lumber

    D patch

22. Which word is an antonym for *bored*?

    F interested

    G tired

    H happy

    J serious

23. Which two words are homophones?

    A dense, dents

    B dunce, dense

    C dance, dances

    D dense, dance

24. Which word fits into both sentences?

    He will _____ for three months to run the marathon.

    The express _____ is the fastest way to get to the city.

    F bus

    G practice

    H train

    J trolley

25. Which phrase means "the head scarf belonging to Katrina"?

    A Katrina head scarf

    B Katrina's head scarf

    C Katrinas' head scarf

    D Katrinas head scarf

26. Which two words are synonyms?

    F ask, reply

    G question, answer

    H answer, reply

    J ask, answer

27. Which two words are antonyms?

    A calm, anxious

    B anxious, worried

    C worried, upset

    D calm, serene

28. Which word defines the underlined word in the sentence? Use context clues.

    Her smile seems <u>phony</u> to me, although many people believe it is genuine.

    F friendly

    G fake

    H true

    J lovely

29. Which word has an *r*-controlled vowel?

    A address

    B patrol

    C coral

    D sprint

30. Which is the correct meaning of *postgame*?

    F a game played in a hurry

    G before a game

    H after a game

    J a change in a game

31. Which word correctly completes the sentence?

    Stir all the lumps out of the cake batter so it won't be _____.

    A lumppy

    B lumpen

    C lumped

    D lumpy

32. Which is the base word of *unmanageable*?

    F manage

    G manly

    H manager

    J managed

Posttest

Read each passage. Then circle the letter of the answer to each question.

The heart is a muscle that acts like a pump to push blood through the body's veins and arteries. The human heart is about the size of a fist and weighs less than a pound. It is divided into two sections, and each section has a different job. The right side takes blood from the body's veins. Blood that passes through this side of the heart has been used by the body. It contains a waste product called carbon dioxide. The right side pumps the blood to the lungs, where the carbon dioxide is removed and oxygen is added. The left side of the heart then collects the clean blood from the lungs and pumps it back to the body through arteries.

1. Which sentence states the main idea of the passage?

  A The heart collects clean blood from the lungs.

  B Used blood contains carbon dioxide.

  C The veins and arteries carry blood.

  D The heart is a muscle with two important jobs.

2. In this passage the heart is compared to a

  F muscle.

  G pump.

  H lever.

  J filter.

Standing in front of the audience, Lupe looked up from her notes and addressed the crowd. "And finally," she said, "I promise that if I am elected to the mayor's council, I will improve communication between city government and every resident." Lupe had imagined this moment since moving to the city five years ago. During the day, she was manager of a savings bank, and in her spare time she volunteered as advisor to a youth organization. She had been involved in many town activities over the years, and she worked hard at everything she did. She had good ideas and the willingness to put them into practice. She had worked hard during her campaign, and now, it was nearly time for the election.

3. What traits best describe Lupe?

  A warm and friendly

  B shy and quiet

  C hardworking and determined

  D loud and obnoxious

4. What do you predict will happen at election time?

  F Lupe will get fired from her bank job.

  G Lupe will vote for another candidate.

  H Lupe will drop out of the election.

  J Lupe will win the election.

> If you ever have the opportunity to see an oarfish, you will never forget it! Oarfish live deep in the warm oceans throughout the tropics and subtropics. These creatures are some of the strangest looking fish that inhabit the sea. Picture a long, skinny, silvery creature up to 30 feet long. It looks more like a snake than a fish. Add what looks like a flowing red mane that extends the entire length of the creature's body. Then imagine two long fins on its underside that look like the oars of a rowboat

5. Which sentence is an opinion?

A Oarfish live deep in the oceans.

B Oarfish can be up to 30 feet long.

C Oarfish are some of the strangest looking fish in the sea.

D Oarfish are skinny, silvery fish.

6. Which style technique does the writer use in the passage?

F short, choppy sentences

G informal language

H descriptive sentences

J dialogue

> (1) Humans are mammals just as dogs, cats, whales, and monkeys are mammals. (2) Many humans keep cats and dogs as pets. (3) Like all mammals, humans have hair, and their internal body temperature remains constant. (4) All female mammals have mammary glands that provide milk to feed their young. (5) What sets humans apart from other mammals? (6) Unlike most mammals, people have hands that can grasp and a brain that can think and reason. (7) Monkeys and apes also have these abilities, but they do not use them together in the same way people do. (8) Only humans put their brains and hands together to create cities and computers and written words. (9) Unlike other mammals, humans have developed written languages.

7. Which sentence is NOT important to understanding the topic?

A sentence 2

B sentence 3

C sentence 7

D sentence 9

8. Which is the best summary of this passage?

F Monkeys can do many of the same things as other mammals can, but they have not developed a written language.

G Humans are mammals just as dogs, cats, whales, and monkeys are mammals, but only humans keep other mammals as pets.

H Humans and other mammals have many things in common. Two things set humans apart. They can create things by using their brains and hands together, and they have written language.

J Humans and other mammals have hair and a constant internal body temperature. All female mammals provide milk for their young.

(1) The tailorbird of south Asia lives up to its name when it makes its nest. (2) First, the bird chooses two leaves that are growing near each other on a tree. (3) Then, with its beak, it punches holes around the edges of the leaves. (4) Using spider silk or long plant fibers, the female begins to stitch the leaves together. (5) She stays between the leaves, while the male stays on the outside. (6) The male protects the territory from other tailorbirds. (7) The female takes two days to complete a cup-shaped pouch for their nest. (8) Once the pouch is finished, the male and female build the nest together. (9) These birds feed on insects, small fruits, berries, and tiny seeds.

9. Which sentence does NOT support the main idea of the passage?

   A sentence 1

   B sentence 3

   C sentence 6

   D sentence 9

10. When tailorbirds make a nest, the first thing they do is

   F feed on tiny seeds.

   G poke a piece of grass through one hole.

   H punch holes around the leaves.

   J choose two leaves.

11. According to the passage, what is the result of the birds' work?

   A two beautiful eggs

   B a trap for insects and spiders

   C a cup-shaped holder for a nest

   D sharper beaks

12. The tailorbird uses spider silk or long plant fibers in the same way that humans use

   F blankets.

   G thread.

   H leaves.

   J eggs.

Cowboys have to be tough and strong to do their jobs. Cowboys are hired hands who round up cattle and drive them to market. Their work takes them over thousands of miles of grasslands and mountains every year. They spend long days in the saddle and often cook and sleep outdoors. With no shelter and only a fire for warmth, cowboys often endure freezing cold nighttime temperatures. In the summer they work a full day in the sun, no matter what the temperature.

13. Which sentence states the main idea of this passage?

   A Cowboys work full days in the hot sun.

   B Cowboys have only fires for warmth.

   C Cowboys are hired hands who round up cattle.

   D Cowboys have to be tough and strong to do their jobs.

14. The author's purpose for writing this passage is to

   F persuade readers to become a cowboy.

   G inform readers about a cowboy's life.

   H entertain readers with a story about the Wild West.

   J describe plants that grow in the grasslands.

Study the graph. Then circle the letter of the answer to each question.

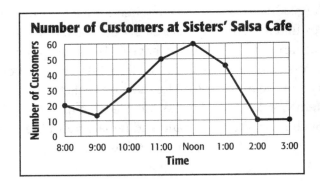

Number of Customers at Sisters' Salsa Cafe

15. At what time were exactly 50 people in the cafe?

  A 9:00 A.M.

  B 11:00 A.M.

  D 8:00 A.M.

  D 3:00 P.M.

16. At what time were the most people in Sisters' Salsa Cafe?

  F 10:00 A.M.

  G 1:00 P.M.

  H noon

  J 11:00 A.M.

17. Based on the graph, you can conclude that

  A the cafe is only open until lunch.

  B the cafe doesn't serve breakfast.

  C the cafe is busiest at lunch time.

  D most customers come to the cafe for dinner.

18. Based on the graph, which statement below is true?

  F More people are in the cafe at 8 A.M. than at 9 A.M.

  G More people are in the cafe at 2 P.M. than at 3 P.M.

  H The same number of people are in the cafe at noon and at 1 P.M.

  J More people are in the cafe at 10 A.M. than at any other time.

The Greek god Zeus sent his daughter Pandora to Earth to be married. As a wedding gift, Zeus gave a beautiful locked box to the couple. He gave them the key but said they must never open ithe box. Pandora could not understand why her father would give her a box if she could not see what was in it. She hated not knowing what was inside. One day Pandora was alone. She took the huge key, put it into the lock, and turned it. Then she opened the box. Before she could stop them, sickness, greed, pain, death, hatred, violence, and war flew out of the box. Pandora slammed the lid shut, but it was too late. These evils have been on Earth ever since.

19. What traits best describe Pandora?

  A honest and obedient

  B curious and disobedient

  C cruel and bitter

  D lazy and forgetful

20. You can conclude that before Pandora opened the box

  F no one on Earth was happy.

  G people on Earth were at war with one another.

  H no one on Earth got sick or died.

  J everyone on Earth died young.

Posttest continued

Study the index. Then circle the letter of the answer to each question.

Index

Behavior, 112–125

  barking, 114

  biting, 120–122

  chewing, 123–125

  crate training, 113–115

  house training, 116–119

  lead training, 112

Commands, 212, 225, 290

Diet, 89–95

  changing of, 91

  special, 93–95

Distemper (disease), 89

Grooming, 150–160

  schedule, 150

  tools for, 155–156

Health (signs of), 201–202

Puppies, 216–224

  buying of, 220

  checklist for, 217

  first days with, 215

  personality types, 222–224

  toys for, 221

---

21. This index most likely comes from

  A a travel guide.

  B a gardening book.

  C a book about dogs.

  D a biology textbook.

22. *Distemper* is the name of a

  F food.

  G disease.

  H behavior.

  J toy.

Read the passage. Then circle the letter of the answer to each question.

---

(1) The term *eagle-eyed* comes from the sharp vision that eagles possess. (2) To begin with, the eagle's eyes are quite large for the bird's size. (3) Human eyes are about the same weight as an eagle's, but an eagle's eye has a much different shape. (4) The back is flatter and larger than the back of our eye. (5) This gives an eagle a much larger image than we can see. (6) An eagle's eyesight can be three to four times stronger than that of humans. (7) That ability is great for spotting potential meals of rabbits and rodents from high up in the sky. (8) Luckily, most people don't need eyesight as sharp as an eagle's.

---

23. What is the author's purpose for writing this passage?

  A to explain why eagles can see better than humans

  B to describe how eagles catch small prey

  C to persuade readers to help save eagles

  D to entertain with a story about eagles

24. What is one way in which eagles and humans are alike?

  F They need strong eyesight to catch small prey.

  G They have eyes that are about the same weight.

  H They have eyes with a flat, large back.

  J They have about the same eyesight.

Read the ad. Then circle the letter of the answer to each question.

Grand Opening Sale!
Frank's Furniture Store

Pay No Interest for 4 Years!*

Deluxe Oak Media Console

Special $399—lowest price in town

42" Computer Desk—Buy NOW!

Big enough for a 17" monitor

Limited quantity—$279

88" Leather Sofa—$599

Beautiful and stylish!

Special prices not available on prior orders.

Limited to stock on hand. Offer good while supplies last.

*No interest charge for 4 years on purchases over $1,000.

125 W. Main, Clark City, IL 60002

---

25. This ad tries to catch the consumer's attention by its

  A large selection.

  B low prices.

  C free delivery policy.

  D hassle-free return policy.

26. When Terri received her credit card bill for a leather sofa, she noticed that interest had been applied to her outstanding balance. What details should Terri have read about the store's policy on interest?

  F Pay No Interest for 4 Years!

  G Limited to stock on hand.

  H Special prices not available on prior orders.

  J No interest charge for 4 years on purchases over $1,000.

27. What statement in the ad is an opinion?

  A Beautiful and stylish!

  B Limited to stock on hand.

  C Special prices not available on prior orders.

  D Lowest price in town.

28. As used in the ad, what does the word *interest* mean?

  F curiosity

  G a financial stake

  H benefit

  J money paid to a lender

Read the workplace document from a home health-care company. Then circle the letter of the answer to each question.

Home Health-care Needs Assessment

To be completed by interviewer.

Name _____   DOB _____

Current living situation of client:

☐ Senior living at home alone.

☐ Senior living at home with spouse.

☐ Senior living at home with family.

Assistance needed with:	Never	Sometimes	Always
Bathing/Showering	☐	☐	☐
Toileting	☐	☐	☐
Dressing/Grooming	☐	☐	☐
Meal preparation/Eating	☐	☐	☐
Medication monitoring	☐	☐	☐
Mobility	☐	☐	☐
Transportation	☐	☐	☐
Shopping	☐	☐	☐

Interview completed by _____   Date: _____

---

29. When might you need to fill out a form like this?

  A when you take a catalog order by phone

  B when you interview a client for home health care

  C when you apply for a job as a hospital aide

  D when you apply for a job as a school bus driver

30. As used in this form, a *senior* is

  F a person holding a high position.

  G a student in the last year of high school.

  H a person of advanced age.

  J an athlete of the highest status.

31. What should you write next to DOB?

  A your date of birth

  B the date that the client was born

  C the number of months you have worked for the company

  D the client's file number in the database

32. As used in this form, what does *current* mean?

  F at the present time

  G the flow of water in a river

  H the flow of electricity through a wire

  J a small fruit

Posttest continued

Read the memo from a day-care company administrator. Then circle the letter of the answer to each question

---

To: New Teachers and Assistant Teachers

From: Smiling Faces Preschool Administration

Date: September 1

Subject: Classroom Management Strategies

Welcome to Smiling Faces Preschool. In our experience, children enter preschool unprepared to follow school rules. Their home behaviors may not be appropriate for school. With appropriate classroom management, children learn good school manners and behaviors.

When a child behaves unacceptably, we suggest you do the following:

- First stop the behavior quickly and follow up with kind words. Do not react with anger, because children should not be afraid of you.
- Make sure to convey that the problem was with the behavior, NOT the child.
- Be respectful and loving no matter what the problem is. Be firm but remain calm and friendly.
- Consequences should be fair, short, and consistent.

If you're not sure how to respond in a given situation, please ask an administrator or an experienced teacher for help.

---

33. Which statement from the memo is a generalization?

A Children enter preschool unprepared to follow school rules.

B Make sure to convey that the problem was with the behavior, NOT the child.

C It's up to you to help children learn school manners and behavior.

D Consequences should be fair, short, and consistent.

34. What would be the effect of a teacher showing anger?

F The children will always behave badly

G The children will fear their teachers.

H The teachers will have to work harder.

J The children will show behaviors that they use at home.

35. What is the first thing to do in response to a child's unacceptable behavior?

A Give a consequence.

B Stop the behavior quickly.

C Respond with kind words.

D Ask an administrator for help.

36. As used in this memo, *firm* means

F solid.

G a business.

H established.

J strong.

Posttest continued

Circle the letter of the word that is spelled correctly and fits in the sentence.

37. I think this is _____ house.

    A they're

    B their

    C there

    D theyr'e

38. _____ shoes are in the hallway?

    F Who's

    G Whoose

    H Whose

    J Who'se

39. You can count on Katt to finish the job; she is _____.

    A relyable

    B reilable

    C reliable

    D relieble

40. We were _____ to attend the concert.

    F hopeing

    G hoping

    H hopeng

    J hoppeng

Circle the letter of the answer to each question.

41. Which word does NOT have a long *a* sound?

    A replay

    B bread

    C waiter

    D mistake

42. Which word is NOT divided correctly into syllables?

    F cer / tain

    G jun / gle

    H wa / gon

    J her / mit

43. Which word is a synonym for *hinder*?

    A help

    B try

    C avoid

    D prevent

44. Which word is the plural of *radish*?

    F radish

    G radishs

    H radishis

    J radishes

45. Which contraction is spelled correctly?

    A shouldn't

    B shudn't

    C shoud'nt

    D should'nt

46. Which word fits into both sentences?

I have a pocket full of _____.

Can you wait while I _____ my clothes?

    F cash

    G change

    H iron

    J wash

47. Which phrase means "the birthplace of my ancestors"?

    A my ancestors birthplace

    B my ancestors's' birthplace

    C my ancestor's birthplace

    D my ancestors' birthplace

48. Which word has two closed syllables?

    F frequent

    G concept

    H slogan

    J fragrant

49. Which word means "appear again"?

   A   appeared

   B   appearance

   C   reappear

   D   disappear

50. What is the meaning of the prefix *bi-*?

   F   three

   G   purchase

   H   two

   J   wheel

51. Which word has an *r*-controlled vowel sound?

   A   rotate

   B   hungry

   C   truffle

   D   merchant

52. Which word has the same vowel sound as *choose*?

   F   groove

   G   stood

   H   brook

   J   hood

53. Which word has three syllables?

   A   militant

   B   mathematical

   C   multiethnic

   D   military

54. Which word is NOT a compound word?

   F   basement

   G   headache

   H   footprint

   J   armchair

55. Which is the base word in the word *prehistoric*?

   A   history

   B   prehistory

   C   historic

   D   histor

56. Which two words are antonyms?

   F   whole, entire

   G   through, threw

   H   messy, sloppy

   J   easy, difficult

57. In which word does *sc* stand for only one sound?

   A   scanner

   B   science

   C   scope

   D   scorn

58. Which word has a soft *g* sound?

   F   grumpy

   G   galaxy

   H   gender

   J   girlish

59. Which word is spelled correctly?

   A   dropping

   B   droping

   C   droppeing

   D   dropiping

60. Which word is a synonym for *unstable*?

   F   strange

   G   wobbly

   H   stable

   J   usual

61. Which word is an antonym for *ancient*?

   A   history

   B   old

   C   elderly

   D   modern

62. Which word has a silent letter?

   F   signal

   G   ringing

   H   sign

   J   string

This posttest was designed to check your mastery of the reading skills studied. Use the key on page 200 to check your answers. Then circle the question numbers that you answered incorrectly and review the practice pages covering those skills. Carefully rework those practice pages to be sure you understand those skills.

Tested Skills	Question Numbers	Practice Pages
Recognize and Recall Details	22	14–17
Understand Stated Concepts	24, 26	22–25
Draw Conclusions	17, 20, 21	30–33
Summarize and Paraphrase	8	38–41
Compare and Contrast	2, 12, 24	46–49
Use Forms	29–32	54–57
Find the Main Idea	1, 13	62–65
Identify Sequence	10, 35	78–81
Use Supporting Evidence	7, 9	86–89
Identify Style Techniques	6	94–97
Make Generalizations	33	102–105
Author's Purpose, Effect, Intention	14, 23	110–113
Read Graphs	15–18	118–121
Predict Outcomes	4	134–137
Identify Cause and Effect	11, 34	142–145
Understand Consumer Materials	25–28	150–153
Recognize Character Traits	3, 19	158–160
Identify Fact and Opinion	5, 27	166–169
Use Indexes	21, 22	174–177
Synonyms/Antonyms	43, 56, 60, 61	37, 45, 84, 92, 141
Context Clues	28, 30, 32, 36, 46	60, 68, 69, 116, 140, 165
Spelling	37–40, 44, 45, 47, 59	21, 28, 44, 52, 61, 85, 100, 109, 117, 124, 125, 148, 156, 157, 172, 181
Phonics/Word Analysis	41, 42, 48–55, 57, 58, 62	20, 21, 28, 29, 36, 44, 52, 53, 60, 68, 84, 92, 93, 100, 101, 108, 116, 124, 140, 148, 149, 156, 164, 172, 173, 180

POSTTEST EVALUATION CHART AND ANSWER KEY continued

	KEY		
1.	D	32.	F
2.	G	33.	A
3.	C	34.	G
4.	J	35.	B
5.	C	36.	J
6.	H	37.	B
7.	A	38.	H
8.	H	39.	C
9.	D	40.	G
10.	J	41.	B
11.	C	42.	H
12.	G	43.	D
13.	D	44.	J
14.	G	45.	A
15.	B	46.	G
16.	H	47.	D
17.	C	48.	G
18.	F	49.	C
19.	B	50.	H
20.	H	51.	D
21.	C	52.	F
22.	G	53.	A
23.	A	54.	F
24.	G	55.	A
25.	B	56.	J
26.	J	57.	B
27.	A	58.	H
28.	J	59.	A
29.	B	60.	G
30.	H	61.	D
31.	B	62.	H